THE TRUTH ABOUT THE IRISH

THE TRUTH ABOUT THE IRISH

TERRY EAGLETON

St. Martin's Griffin
New York

www.stn

ISBN 0-312-25488-1 (hc)
ISBN 0-312-26403-8 (pbk)

First published in Ireland by New Island Books

First St. Martin's Griffin Edition: March 2001

10 9 8 7 6 5 4 3 2 1

For
Michael Henry

THE TRUTH ABOUT THE IRISH

A to Z of the Irish

Y ou have just arrived at Dublin airport from Sydney or Sacramento, Salisbury or Siena. Now you need transport downtown. Follow the signs in the airport marked 'Donkey Carts' and you will come to a spacious field thronged with hand-made wooden carts, each with a small donkey in harness. For the price of a glass of whiskey, a driver in a green smock will jog you down the leafy lanes which wind their way to the city centre, singing a Gaelic love song and swigging from a bottle of poteen, an illegal, mind-numbing alcohol distilled from potatoes. From the mud cabins by the roadside, simple-hearted peasants will strew shamrock at your feet, shouting 'Long life to your Honour!' Lithe young damsels in green mini-skirts will beckon you alluringly with one hand while strumming a harp with the other. When you enter the ancient gate of the city, a band of kilted pipers playing 'Danny Boy' will be on hand to offer you a hearty Irish welcome. You will be ceremonially lowered under a gallon-sized vat of Guinness, which custom ordains that you should empty in three minutes flat. If you fail to down the stuff in time, you will fall victim to an ancient Irish curse and your credit cards will be turned into toads.

Forget that last paragraph. It was a pack of lies. There are no donkeys at Dublin airport. In fact there are precious few

donkeys left in Ireland at all.[1] There are no simple peasants
either – partly because there are no peasants anyway, partly
because peasants are about as simple as the Theory of
Relativity. The second great disappointment of your visit is
just about to hit you: *Ireland is just as modern as wherever it is
you came from.* Well, more or less. Unless you're an Eskimo,
of course.

(The first great disappointment, by the way, is that it's
raining. As it will be tomorrow. And the next day...) The
Irish drive cars, play the stock market and wear trousers
rather than kilts. The country has computers, Big Macs,
Japanese cuisine, bad American movies on TV, quite a few
millionaires, generous tax breaks for foreign investors, a
thriving film industry known as Paddywood, and more
lawyers than leprechauns. The cow is no longer the unit of
exchange, as it was in early medieval Ireland. If you're
American, and came here to escape all that, don't forget that
some of it is because of YOU. You want the Irish to be
different, and they want to be like you. The first thing you'll
need if you come to live in Dublin is not a charm to ward off
the fairies but a burglar alarm to ward off the felons. Drug-
related crime is rampant in deprived areas of the city. Social
decay blights both the cities and the countryside on a large
scale.

So the bad news for romantic tourists is that Ireland is up-
to-date. As someone once said, Ireland has lost the

---

[1] FACT TO IMPRESS YOUR FRIENDS (hereafter FIF): Not
many people know that donkeys were useful in Ireland because of
the way they put their feet down. They do this in a pattern different
from that of a horse, which allows them to move across bogland in
a gliding movement. If the Irish had used horses, they might have
sunk without trace.

leprechaun but found the pot of gold. Actually, though, that's not the whole truth either. In fact the whole truth about Ireland is as elusive a commodity as Irish coal. It *is* a modern nation, but it modernised only recently, and at the moment is behaving rather like a lavatory attendant who has just won the lottery. Many features of the country remain fairly traditional. Homosexuality, for instance, was only made legal in 1993, and abortion, except when the mother's life is at risk, is still against the law.

Some aspects of Dublin are still more like Cairo than Cambridge. You will find cars parked on the sidewalks and the streets ankle-deep in litter. You'll even find one or two mosques. As in Cairo, unemployed men hang around to help you park your car in return for a tip. Orange traffic lights in Dublin mean Go, whereas red ones mean Stop if you feel in the mood and fancy a breather. The city has horses and carts, five-year-old beggars, gaudy religious icons and statues of national freedom fighters. Spitting in the street is a national pastime. People ride bicycles at breakneck speed down crowded pavements.

Dublin's main thoroughfare, O'Connell Street, has declined from its eighteenth-century grandeur into a dingy collection of fast-food joints. One critic called its architectural style 'neon-classical'. The street contains statues of the Irish politicians Daniel O'Connell and Charles Stewart Parnell, and used to have one to Lord Nelson too, before the IRA blew it up in the 1960s. The Irish poet W.B. Yeats remarked that the street therefore commemorated three of history's best-known adulterers. You won't find a Casbah in the city, but you will find Temple Bar, a bohemian quarter of art galleries, boutiques and veggie cafés where the Gilded Youth of the city come out at night to stare at each other. There were 26 stag (bachelor) parties there each weekend before they were banned, and 36,000 people troop through the place every day.

Americans in particular tend to find Ireland unhygienic, inefficient, alarmingly laid-back about smoking and ill-provided with showers. You can drink on the streets, drop your empty can at your feet, and lie down for a quick snooze on the sidewalk, without anybody much objecting. Despite all that, the place looks a lot more like Boston than Baghdad.

So was your journey really necessary? If it was the exotic you were after, shouldn't you have headed for Papua New Guinea instead? Pause, however, before you climb back on the plane. Why not check in your myths at the airport and enjoy your vacation all the more? Dublin may be the shabbiest capital in Europe, as one critic has called it, with a lot of run-down, drug-infested housing estates. But it's also a vibrant, talkative, sociable, effervescent city, with the odd touch of carnival about it. And the Irish Tourist Board isn't even paying me to say so. The Irish may be in the grip of the success ethic these days, but they still take more time out for friendship and generally messing around than most other nations.

The point is that the Irish were never really an industrialised nation, and so have never been deeply affected by the disciplines which all that brings with it. They are leaping from being a largely rural nation to being a high-tech one, skipping the industrial stage in between. They still don't make a religion of work as some countries do, or get up at six o'clock in the morning to run eight miles, swallow a gallon of grapefruit juice and take three showers in a row. The very idea would horrify most of them. They are less flashy than the States and less frigid than England.

The rest of this book will be devoted to examining some familiar images of Ireland, to find out how much truth there is in them. Two general points before we start. First, by 'Ireland', we mean the Republic of Ireland; Northern Ireland is a very different place, and would need a book to itself. Second, some people think it vaguely racist to speak of 'the Irish' or 'the Ukranians', as though they were all the same. There are indeed very different kinds of Irish people, as this book hopes to show. But people who share the same conditions of life for a long time also tend to develop certain cultural habits in common. It's as wrong-headed to overlook this as it is to imagine that one Irish person is just a clone of another. I once saw a TV documentary about Peru in which an army officer barked at his men: 'Men, never forget that you are Peruvians'. This is funny, at least to us non-Peruvians, since 'being Peruvian' doesn't signify much at all. (Maybe it doesn't for the Peruvians either). It would be rather like saying: 'Never forget that you come from East Cheam' or 'Always remember that you are from South Bend, Indiana'. The Irish, on the other hand, have one of the most vivid public images in the world, though a remarkably self-contradictory one. They are seen as childlike and devious, genial and aggressive, witty and thick-headed, quick and slow, eloquent and blundering, laid-back and hot-tempered, dreamy and earthy, lying and loyal. So either they're schizoid, or they defy the laws of logic.

We begin, of course, with ALCOHOL – the AARDVARK of the Irish people.

ALCOHOL

Everyone knows that the Irish are among the booziest nations on earth. In fact, this may be a myth. On one reckoning, the Irish have the lowest per capita consumption of alcohol, or 'gargle' as they sometimes call it, of any of the

European Union countries except Greece and Italy. Between 20% and 30% of Irish men and women are teetotal. It may not look that way on a Saturday night in the centre of Dublin, but it's true. Nations like Ireland with a tradition of heavy drinking also tend to produce temperance movements, just as nations which suffer from obesity also produce health freaks. The Irish understand about drink, but they also understand about abstinence, and are rather less likely to get upset if you refuse a drink than they might in Frankfurt or Florence. Anyway, the image of the Irish as heavy drinkers was often based on Irish immigrants abroad rather than those at home. And immigrants have sorrows they need to drown.

Even so, the abstinence tradition may account in part for the surprisingly low per capita consumption. A lot of the Irish don't drink at all, while the rest of them selflessly make up for this national deficiency by downing the stuff in generous quantities. It's also true that drinking at home isn't an Irish custom. In 1994, the Irish spent a total of £2.46 billion on alcohol, which works out at an average of close to £1,000 for each adult member of the population. And if you exclude the teetotallers and the children from your calculations, Ireland shoots back to the top of the European alcoholic league table.

A lot of Irish pubs run at a loss. It's true that by 1914 Guinness's brewery was the largest in the world, and by far the biggest employer in the country.[2] A lot of the Irish worked hard in order to render the rest of the country legless.

---

[2] FIF: If you think Guinness is as Irish as shamrock, the bad news is that these days it's part of a multinational corporation, in which the Guinness family themselves own less than 2% of the shares, and have no member on the board of directors.

The brewery still exports nearly a million pints of stout a day. But today some of the Irish are drinking less, not least because of the fearful price of the stuff. Heavy drinking remains an Irish custom – I have an Irish friend who regards drinking ten pints of stout a day as purely routine – but it's by no means a universal pastime. This is partly because a lot of Irish drunkenness was a mark of the low self-esteem of a colonised nation. There wasn't much else to do, and it was an escape from the poverty and hopelessness around you. Next to emigration, it was the quickest way out.

There was a brisk black market trade in poteen, which the British banned in 1831. The word 'poteen' indicates not so much a particular kind of alcohol, as any spirit distilled illegally. It could be made from potatoes, grain, sugar or even treacle. It's still furtively distilled in Ireland, though if you're caught you can be fined up to £1,000. The sin of brewing poteen had traditionally to be confessed to a bishop, a priest being too lowly a mortal to deal with such a moral enormity. There is, however, a commercial brand of the stuff these days, though forbidden hooch tastes sweeter. To test whether poteen is drinkable, the best plan is to set it on fire. If it burns with a purple tinted flame, it might just possibly not be poisonous; if it shows a red flame, it probably is. If it explodes and burns all your hair off, don't worry: drinking the stuff has far worse effects.

Now that the nation is more on its feet, however, it's less often on its back. Though reports of the Irish in ancient times mention their liking for strong drink, as well as their fighting spirit, impulsive nature and love of fantasy. And though the more materially successful of the Irish may have cut their alcohol intake, drink remains a refuge for the swollen army of the poor. Wine remains fairly unpopular, at a mere five bottles per head a year, while stout is still an alcoholic front runner. 'Stout' actually means 'strong', and is short for the phrase 'stout porter', which was the most popular drink in nineteenth-century Britain. Porter was a darker coloured beer, so-called because it was said to be popular with London market porters.

The worst pubs in Ireland, like the best ones, aren't just for drinking in. The pubs to avoid are those which have really turned themselves into fast-food joints, with piped music, fruit machines, and huge TV screens to kill off the conversation. The best pubs are those in which drinking is part of socialising, arguing, live music sessions or just taking some time off to reflect, rather like the old-style Parisian café. Most Irish pubs welcome children, as most English ones don't. The Irish are genuinely fond of children, unlike those nations which dote on kids, but not other people's. The English go all weak at the knees if you wheel a badger down the street, but not a baby. The Irish, by contrast, were telling opinion pollsters a few years ago that they believed that four or five children make an ideal family unit, which is way out of line with the rest of Europe. It's also way out of line with their current practice.

Irish and English pubs are alike in that if you just want to nurse your drink undisturbed, people will leave you alone. If you don't, then they'll talk you into the ground. It isn't really acceptable to refuse the offer of a drink in Ireland, though you don't have to choose alcohol any more. You must return the favour and buy drinks for those who have treated you. The hospitable Irish frown on anyone who doesn't pull their social weight. Irish people may refuse food or drink when you first invite them, but this is usually just politeness, and you must ask them again. Some think that this comes from the days when there wasn't really enough food to be shared. The Irish law of hospitality ordained that, even so, when a stranger visited your cabin, you had to share your scanty supply of food with him, and if necessary give him shelter for the night. Even today, the Irish might say 'I've had my dinner' when invited to sit down to the family meal, though it may not be exactly true.

When the closing time ordained by Irish law arrives in a pub, the barman may shout 'Come on now, the Gardai (police) are outside', or 'Don't you know your homes are being burgled?' Nobody will move, knowing these to be Irish fictions.

In Ireland as elsewhere, drinking alcohol is strictly confined to certain times and occasions. You drink when

you're sad, but also when you're happy; when you're bored, but also when something pleasant happens; when you're alone to cheer yourself up, but also in company. Drinking is okay when on holiday, but also at work to relieve the pressures. It's best to confine it to meal times, but also good to drink between meals when you're feeling at a loose end. By restricting your drinking in this way, you will be in no danger of overdoing it. The Irish tend not to say 'he was drunk', but 'drink had been taken'. This is a pleasant way of implying that you were drunk but you didn't do it yourself.

ANGLO-IRISH RELATIONS

The British owned Ireland for centuries, but nowadays many of them never set foot in the place. These two facts may not be unconnected. The English love to take their holidays in Scotland and Wales, and more and more of them crowd over to Dublin for a boozy weekend. Most of these see no more of the place than their own out-of-focus feet, which they could have viewed more cheaply back home. They also tend to pronounce the name of the country as 'Eye-land', since the English, unlike the Irish, have a problem in sounding their *R's*. But a good number of them abandon this uniquely beautiful corner of Europe to the French and Germans, who have to travel further to get there. The British do in fact form a high proportion of tourists to Ireland, but 'Funny thing, but I've never actually been to Ireland', is a remarkably common English comment.[3] This is partly because most of what the

---

[3] FIF: Ireland now has more tourists than residents. Tourist numbers are running at around 5½ million a year, compared to a population of about 3.8 million.

English see about Ireland on television is people bombing each other in the North. So they're afraid of getting their heads shot off in the wilds of Connemara, even if statistically speaking they have more chance of being savaged by a sheep.

But it also springs from centuries of seeing the Irish as colonial inferiors. The definition of 'Irish' in the Oxford English Dictionary used to include bad-temper and illogicality. English attitudes to the Irish are a bizarre mixture of affection, uneasiness, condescension and hostility. They tend to find the Irish quaint, feckless, aggressive and unruly, and can never quite decide whether they find this enormously enjoyable or downright distasteful. If you have studied the ambiguous reaction of people in a public place to some uproarious drunk singing his head off and falling about, then you have witnessed something of the mixture of wariness and warmth, embarrassment and envy, with which the English treat their Celtic ex-colonials.

Though some aspects of British rule in Ireland were fairly enlightened, the British sometimes treated the Irish shabbily, even brutally, when they owned the place. But it isn't fashionable to say this in Ireland at the moment, for a number of reasons. First, because the Irish are afraid that saying so might give comfort to the IRA, who have little support in the Irish Republic. Second, because the Irish and the British are now partners in the European Union, and some of the Irish want to put all that squalid history behind them. They're much too busy turning a fast buck and proving that they're as cybernetic as anyone else to want to be reminded of it. Thirdly, because the Irish population is largely made up of young people, many of whom find history, politics and nationalism as boring as algebra or Julie Andrews. So don't think that you'll ingratiate yourself with the Irish by slagging off the British. This will be music to the ears of nationalists, but it's hard to know at a glance who is a nationalist and who isn't. At least it is in the Irish Republic. In Northern Ireland, some Protestant Unionists claim they can spot Catholic nationalists by how close-set their eyes are, and vice versa.

On the whole, the Irish get on better with the Americans, with whom they have an historic relationship, than they do with the British, with whom they have an historic relationship some of them would prefer to forget. In fact one major difference between the Irish and the English is that the Irish like the Americans, whereas the English, on the whole, don't. The open, free-and-easy Irish life-style is much closer to American culture than it is to the reserved, hierarchical British. No other nation in its long history has been as generous to the Irish as the USA. In the nineteenth century, some villages in the west of Ireland were kept afloat by the New York Police Department. Without the money sent home by emigrant New York policemen, they would have sunk without trace. These days, the USA helps to keep the place afloat by tourism, as well as by industrial investment, which is rather more useful to the Irish than secret shipments of arms.

After a long, turbulent marriage, the Irish and the English were finally divorced in 1922, when Ireland became partly independent. Nowadays they react to each other with something like the edginess of divorced partners, at once intimate and estranged. Like divorced couples, they know each other far better than anyone else does, yet never really got the hang of each other at all. Ireland was always too close to Britain to be ignored and too alien to be understood. Since the Irish are white English-speaking westerners, the British have tended to see them as much like themselves, ignoring the cultural differences between them. They forget that the Irish only spoke English because the English occupied their territory and taught it to them.

It's a sign of the oddness of Anglo-Irish relations that there's no word today for the group of islands which includes Great Britain and the whole of Ireland. It isn't the British Isles, since the Republic of Ireland isn't British. When all of Ireland was British-ruled, the whole area was known as the United Kingdom of Great Britain and Ireland. Since the south became independent, this has shrunk to the United Kingdom of Great Britain and Northern Ireland, or just the United Kingdom. But no single geopolitical term covers the entire landmass. There has been an attempt afoot to introduce the term IONA – Islands of the North Atlantic – which cannily combines Celtic mystique and geopolitical modernity. It's also odd to speak of the Republic of Ireland as the 'south', since some of it – Donegal, for instance – is actually in the north. A lot of things in Ireland are topsy-turvy. What you call various bits of Ireland tends to reveal your politics. 'Eire' is still the official name for the Republic, but an Irish nationalist wouldn't use it. It would imply accepting that the island is divided into two for all eternity, so that that one piece of it requires a special name other than simply Ireland. Language in Ireland is a political minefield: whether you call a certain northern city Derry or Londonderry depends on your religious and political views. Catholic nationalists call it Derry, while Protestant Unionists call it Londonderry.

ARAN ISLANDS

These are both real and mythical at the same time. The three barren, beautiful islands lie thirty miles off the coast of Galway, and one of them, Inishmore, contains the fort of

Dun Aengus, which has been called the most magnificent ancient monument in Europe. Half of it may have fallen into the ocean, but this carelessness doesn't really detract from its splendour. The islands are strewn with the ruins of churches, High Crosses, hermitages, round towers and prehistoric forts, and the soil was artificially created by the impoverished islanders out of sand and seaweed. It's a community of Irish-speaking fisher-folk, some of whom still wear their famous *pampooties* or hide shoes. Many of them over the years have been lost to the sea. If you're looking for the End of the World and the Garden of Eden rolled into one, search no further. In fact if you search any further you'll drown.

Over the years, the Aran islands have attracted as many visiting anthropologists as the Amazon basin. In fact some of the Aran folk used to wonder whether the world beyond their islands was populated entirely by linguists and anthropologists. There are also those on the mainland who believe that the islands were specially constructed by the Irish Tourist Board to give anthropologists something to write about, and that the natives are actually out-of-work actors from Dublin who talk any old gobbledy-gook to impress the tourists with their wise Gaelic ways. Rumour has it that the islands are rolled up when the tourist season ends and towed into Galway, where workmen chip away at the rocks to make them look a bit more rugged. At the turn of this century, many ardent Irish nationalists made their way from middle-class Dublin, notebooks and Irish dictionaries in hand, to savour this unspoilt bit of old Ireland. The islanders found it hard to give these enthusiasts their full attention, intent as they were on how to get off these goddam rocks to a decent life on the mainland.

Speaking of anthropologists, the story is told of an American anthropologist who was collecting folk tales out west. Stumbling upon a village whose inhabitants seemed to have an unusually plentiful supply of these tales, and to be well practised in reciting them, he asked an old woman, bent and withered in her black shawl, why she thought this might be. 'I think, sir', she replied, 'that it may have something to do with the post-war influx of American anthropologists'.

Think twice before you buy yourself an Aran sweater. For one thing, not many people look good in them. You have to have the right shape and colouring. For another thing, wearing an Aran sweater as a tourist in Ireland would be like a British tourist wearing a stars-and-stripes suit on Park Avenue, or a Bolivian sporting a bowler hat and pinstripe trousers in Trafalgar Square. But if you want to make an eejit (Irish for idiot) of yourself, nobody's going to stop you.

BEAUTY

Is Ireland one of the most beautiful spots on the planet? Indeed it is, but small thanks to the Irish. They are notorious for their lack of visual sense, as opposed to their breath-taking music and magnificent literature. Hence all that ankle-high litter and streets awash with saliva. The Irish poet Paul Durcan wrote of the restaurant in Dublin's national art gallery that the only problem with it was that you had to go through the art gallery to get at it (but he was only joking). A few decades ago, seized by a frenzied fit of collective vandalism, the Irish started pulling down some of their priceless Georgian buildings and had to be forcibly restrained.

Some think that this casualness comes from Ireland's colonial history. In some ways the Irish have behaved as though their country isn't their own, because for a long time it wasn't. It belonged, in case you weren't paying attention, to Britain, and a war-torn bit of it in the north still does. But attitudes are now changing: polls suggest that the Irish these days feel more personally able to influence political matters than some other European nations. Traditionally, however, the Irish were too poverty-stricken to bother their heads about beauty. Landscapes were for sowing with potatoes, not for staring at. To excel in architecture you need leisure, resources and stability, and these in Ireland have been in short supply. Music and literature, on the other hand, can survive through periods of disruption, which the country has witnessed in plenty.

The Irish are poor town-planners, partly because as a rural people they never built many towns for themselves. Most of their main urban settlements, like Dublin, Limerick, Wexford and Waterford, were built by the marauding Vikings, who were handy with a hammer. The very name 'Ireland' is of Scandinavian origin. Dublin is a fairly young city as European settlements go, built in the ninth century. The oldest city in Ireland is Armagh, which is also the traditional centre of church authority. Dublin was a way-station for the Vikings as they sailed to Africa to engage in the slave trade. The Vikings helped to preserve a lot of precious Irish objects by a technique known as stealing: they kept them in treasure-hoards which we stumbled upon later. The real centres of Gaelic civilisation in the Middle Ages were monasteries, not towns. Irish villages are mostly drab looking places, usually with a single wide main street and a thin huddle of houses and pubs. The width of the main street was useful for moving cattle, as well as for moving British troops to flush out Irish rebels.

BEAG

The Irish word for 'small'. Since it sounds quite like 'big', especially as the Northern Irish pronounce that word, this caters to the prejudice that the Irish get things the wrong way round. Irishmen are on average bigger than Englishmen, or at least they were in the nineteenth century. We know this from military records of soldiers' physiques, since an enormous number of the British army were Irish. Killing other people was preferable to starving to death yourself. Michael Collins and Eamon de Valera, the two great leaders of the Irish independence movement, were known respectively as the Big Fellow and the Long Fellow. De Valera, who was gaunt and gangly, was once described as looking like something uncoiled from the Book of Kells.[4] The smallest thing in Ireland used to be the fairies. You had to call them affectionate names like 'the good people' ('little people' is a modern invention), otherwise they might turn nasty and inflame your joints with rheumatism, blight your crops or kidnap your babies. This is the earliest recorded form of alien abduction. An old Irish woman who was asked whether she believed in the fairies replied that she didn't, but they were there anyway. Nowadays the smallest thing in Ireland is your bank balance after a night on the town.

Another confusing aspect of the country is that what the Irish call 'Big Houses' are often not all that big. The Big House was where the land-owning gentry, usually of English origin, used to live, and you can still find some splendid ones in existence, though many were burned down by the IRA during the war of independence. ('Who should I say called?'

---

[4] FIF: Another bit of Ireland which would be enormous if uncoiled is the coastline, which would stretch most of the way to New York.

one frosty Big House butler is said to have asked the looters, as they dashed through the front door with half the furniture.) Some Big House landlords owned thousands of acres and rented them out to hundreds of small tenants. Their bailiffs would carry weapons around with them, especially when they went to collect the rent, since rent-collecting for some mysterious reason was a practice displeasing to the Irish farmers. This may just have been because a lot of them were living in near-destitution and couldn't even afford one pair of shoes amongst their twelve children, let alone to pay the landlord good money for the privilege of starving on two or three stony acres of soil.

Back in the eighteenth century, the Anglo-Irish landlords were rumoured to be a fairly riotous bunch. A lot of them passed their time hunting, duelling, smashing each others' skulls, throwing each other out of windows, and claiming sexual favours from their tenants' daughters. They imported into Ireland a phenomenal amount of booze – around 15 million gallons of wine a year in the late eighteenth century – and guzzled it all themselves. Some of them were fairly impoverished, while others ate more in a week than their impoverished tenants ate in a year. A fair number of them were absentees, living it up in London and hardly ever clapping eyes on their Irish estates. There were plenty of humane, conscientious landlords; but too many of them were a brawling, foul-mouthed, belligerent bunch who understood horses far better than humans (see HORSES). Every now and then they got assassinated by an aggrieved tenant. The Irish poet Louis McNeice described them as having 'nothing but an insidious bonhomie, an obsolete bravado and a way with horses'. A lot of the Anglo-Irish gentry left the country when it became independent in 1922, fearing that there would be no place for them in the new regime. But a remnant of them lives on, gentle eccentrics in crumbling mansions with leaky roofs, some precious portraits and a few stuffed heads of peasants on the wall to remind them of their past glory.

BEGORRAH

Nobody in Ireland has ever been known to use this word, just as no American actually says 'Jeepers Creepers', no Brits say 'Top hole, old sport' and no self-respecting Scot says 'Hoots, mon'. 'Begorrah' is as much a myth as Old King Cole. It's true that in the days when one Dublin theatre, the Gate, was run by a famously homosexual couple, and another, the Abbey, put on Irish plays, the two places were known as Sodom and Beggorah.[5] But if you hear anyone say 'Bergorrah' during your stay, you can be sure he's an undercover agent for the Irish Tourist Board, pandering to your false expectations. That the Irish don't like disappointing their visitors, however, is *not* on the whole a myth. If they tell you the place you're looking for is just round the corner, it probably means that it's three bus-rides away. (If you're an American, remember that in Irish-English as in English-English, '*right* down the road' means just a long way down the road, not a little way).

---

[5] FIF: The site on which the Abbey theatre stands today was previously occupied by a morgue. Some think that this accounts for the lifeless quality of some of the acting. Fittingly, when the old theatre was demolished in 1961, the bricks were used to lay a pathway in a cemetery. The Abbey was the first state-sponsored theatre in the English-speaking world.

BLARNEY

'The greatest talkers since the ancient Greeks', was how the Dubliner Oscar Wilde described the Irish, with himself well in mind. This doesn't apply to all of them. In Ireland as anywhere else, there are people who can't put two words together, especially if the two words in question are 'another Guinness?' But the Irish have a strong oral tradition of folklore and storytelling, which runs back to their very early history. Irish literature is full of puns, riddles, word play and fantasy. Some people relate the Irish gift for speech to their traditional poverty, since words cost nothing, and verbal fantasy was a way of escaping harsh reality. A wealth of words could compensate for a lack of food. Others relate it to the Irish pastime of bamboozling their British masters. The word 'blarney' derives from the sixteenth-century Earl of Blarney, who like other Irish chieftains at the time was asked to declare his loyalty to a foreign monarch, England's Queen Elizabeth I. He gave such a florid speech that nobody could tell whether he was submitting or rebelling.

But there are also harsher critics of the Irish, including some of the Irish themselves, who see blarney and bluster as part of their chronic inability to face up to the truth about themselves. (The Irish scholar John Pentland Mahaffy observed that he was only ever whipped once as a child, for telling the truth.) On this view, it was always easier to blame the British for your shortcomings than to shoulder responsibility for them yourself. If you were carried legless every night from the pub, the obvious reason was British imperialism. On this theory, blarney is bound up with a gap between the realities of Irish life and the hypocritical appearances. For example: the official name of the state is Eire, but hardly anybody uses it. The official language is

Irish, but the vast majority of the population don't speak it. Politicians often preface their public speeches with a few words of Irish, but this is about as meaningful as clearing your throat. There are laws in plenty, but it's customary in some quarters to be fairly casual about them. The constitution has traditionally laid claim to sovereignty over the North, and lots of the Irish tout nationalist sentiments; but the North is also a pain in the neck and a global embarrassment which many of them would rather ignore. Ireland is a deeply Catholic country, yet opinion polls suggest that, when it comes to morality, around 78% of its people believe in ignoring the church and following their own conscience. The Irish flock devoutly to mass, but a lot of them believe that the Irish Catholic church is dying slowly on its feet. More and more of them condone sexual permissiveness, while continuing to hold traditional Christian values in other areas of life. For a long time there was no divorce, but people co-habit quite openly, including the present Prime Minister. There's a wealth of lip-service paid to tradition, but it mustn't interfere with the pragmatic business of turning a quick *punt*. All of this is what one politician has called the Irish people's unwillingness to cast aside symbols while ignoring them in practice.

Further contradictions abound. Traditional Irish culture is to be celebrated, but most people prefer to watch Australian soap opera on television. The Irish love their country, but have invested an immense amount of energy in getting out of it. Family values are highly respected, but this didn't stop some of the Irish recommending emigration, which involves the break-up of the family, as a solution to the nation's ills. The nation is proud of its new-found self-assurance, but most of its economic buoyancy flows from foreign sources. It's also proud to have shaken off its subservience to Britain, so instead bows its knee to Brussels. The Irish want to be a distinctive nation, and at the same time want to be just like everyone else. By far the greater part of Ireland is rural, but it's chic in some quarters to sneer at the benighted countryside. The Irish take pride in the beauty of their landscape, but have turned a blind eye to environmental pollution.

To return to the topic of blarney: like a lot of subject peoples, the Irish used speech as a way of hiding their true thoughts from their rulers. Some Irish small farmers would pay extravagant compliments to their English landlord, and then, when night fell, would creep out and burn his crops. If the Irish are splendid writers, it's partly because writing doesn't require a lot of expensive equipment, like, say, opera or symphonies. It's also because the language which most of them now write in, English, isn't their native tongue, so that they sometimes write it with a haunting strangeness. One traditional way of getting out of Ireland was to talk or write your way out. Most Irish writers ended up in London, since Ireland didn't have much of a publishing industry, and some of the Irish became eloquent orators in the House of Commons. Deprived of wealth, the Irish were forced to live by their wits. Which takes us back to Oscar Wilde, one of the greatest Irish wits of all.

B & B

You'll see a lot of these signs on houses in Ireland, meaning 'Bar and Brothel'. Knock boldly on the front door, and don't be fooled by the homely, respectable appearance of the Madame who opens it. Despite that flowery apron and bun of grey hair, she's seen it all. Just describe to her straight out your weirdest sexual fantasies, and she will be glad to oblige.

BODHRÁN

(Pronounced *bow-rawn*). A large, round, thick-skinned object, usually tight, which you have to hit with a stick to get anything out of. Elsewhere in the world, this is known as a husband. In Ireland it's a musical instrument, a kind of outsize tambourine played with the hand or with a knobbed bone. You'll see it in pubs, along with other traditional Irish instruments such as fiddles, banjos, tin whistles and the *uilleann* pipes, which unlike Scottish bagpipes are operated by the elbow (see MUSIC). You won't, however, see the harp, which despite being a national emblem isn't often used in traditional Irish music. They're not easy to drag through the pub door. Like many other things in Ireland, the *bodhrán* (which actually means 'a deaf person') isn't really as traditional as it looks, having come into its own only at the end of the last century. 'A botheration of *bodhráns*' is the collective noun.

BOGS

One sixth of Ireland consists of bogland, a higher proportion than any other European country except Finland. Most of the bogs are concentrated in the midlands and the west. For the visitor, a bog is just a bog: a wild, harsh, damp, dismal stretch of ground which it's best to drive through as quickly as possible before it starts to chase after you (see below). To the educated eye of the geographer, however, bogs divide into various types, such as 'raised' and 'blanket' bogs. Blanket bogs, as the word suggests, are huge, treeless, fairly flat expanses of land in areas of high rainfall. Raised bogs, which occur in areas of lower rainfall, are smaller, richer in vegetation, and grow upwards in a dome-like shape.

Irish bogs may look unenticing, but without them the Irish would have been much more vulnerable to military invasion. Mountains and bogs together made conquering the country as a whole a well-nigh impossible task. Bogs also made the Irish less vulnerable to cold. The peat or 'turf' hacked from them with a spade known as a *'slean'* was for centuries the main fuel supply for most of the population. Nowadays, turf-cutting, rather less romantically, is a large-scale commercial industry, and on your travels you may see workmen cutting turf with machines and loading it into carts.

Depleted over the years, Irish bogs are now major conservation areas, not least because of their world-wide importance as geological features. They are now becoming tourist and recreational resources as well as industrial and scientific ones. But bogs are also part of the Irish imagination, as places where nature can be experienced at its greatest intensity. For a people traditionally attached to the land but nowadays increasingly urbanised, they represent a precious heritage. Bogs are a spiritual as well as material resource, invaluable for educational, scientific and aesthetic reasons as well as for feeding your fire.

Bogs also act as museums, preserving vital evidence from the past. Over the years, they have thrown up all kinds of buried implements and utensils, not to speak of the odd corpse, all in an uncannily well-preserved state. They are time capsules, in which wooden objects or articles of clothing which would otherwise have decayed are stored in tip-top condition. Some of these artefacts were probably just lost, others may have been buried for ritual purposes, while others were probably meant to be recovered. They may have been buried by our remote ancestors with a benevolent eye on future generations of archaeologists. (There is a piece of knotted rope in the National Museum in Cairo whose function archaeologists used to puzzle over, until they concluded that it was probably just their predecessors' thoughtful way of letting them know how they tied a knot.) Bogs also preserve millions of grains of pollen, which allow scientists to reconstruct the flora and fauna of past ages. We can learn a lot from them about the forests which once thickly covered the country.

If bogs have haunted the Irish imagination, it may be partly because they reveal the past as still present. With a bog and its buried contents, the past is no longer behind you, but palpably beneath your feet. A secret history is stacked just a few feet below the modern world in which you're standing. This, in fact, has been one way in which the history-plagued Irish have sometimes conceived of their past – not as a set of events over and done with, but as something still alive in the present. There is a road-sign in County Donegal which reads 'To the Flight of the Earls', an event which took place in the early seventeenth century. This is rather like having an English road-sign announcing 'To the Industrial Revolution', or an American one directing you to the War of Independence.

Objects preserved in bogs are caught in a kind of living death, and this sense of death as part of life has been a theme of traditional Irish culture (see WAKE). It's there too in the Irish love of the ghost story, in which the shades of the dead slip into the living present. The country is full of ruins and spectres, of a past which won't lie down, of those who perished in war or famine refusing to be laid decently to rest and returning to lay siege to the living (see DRACULA). Over the past few decades in Northern Ireland, religious conflicts which date from the seventeenth century have been slogging it out on the streets. What seems to have been buried safely out of sight is thrust suddenly to the surface, like a corpse rearing up from a bog. Irish literature has often envisaged time as moving in cycles, rather than striding confidently forward to some brave new world. There is too burdensome a weight of the past in Ireland. But if you try to sweep it under the carpet, it will only return to plague you again. It's a thought worth cherishing for those tourists who love to come to Ireland because everything's so nice and old.

It's a myth that bogs just lie there inertly without stirring. Most of the time they do, but occasionally they have been known to shift around. Some years ago, a motorist was driving along the north coast of County Mayo when he was alarmed to see a bog advancing slowly towards him along the road. This was a result of land subsidence, but word soon got around that, after years of people leaving the land for foreign parts, the land itself was now desperately trying to emigrate.

Bogs aren't the only thing in Ireland which shift round when they ought to stay still. The same applies to some holy wells, which have been known to hop from one field to another when nobody's looking. A holy well in really good shape, one whose water will cure your migraine or lumbago, can leap several fields overnight. Statues of the Virgin are also sometimes given to jiggling mysteriously around. Some of the more athletic ones have attracted huge crowds of spectators, all patiently waiting for the statue to shake a leg or throw them a wink. This isn't quite as funny as it sounds. Incidents like this tend to occur in poor rural regions, where loneliness, frustration and a yearning for a spot of excitement can easily throw up the odd miracle. It's true that when the Virgin puts in an appearance, she tends to speak in rather vague, woolly terms about world peace, like a UN Secretary General. But dancing statues and hopping wells can also speak of a desire for a better world, and nobody who has had a taste of the drearier sides of Irish life can be surprised at that.

BIFFO/BUFFALO

Irish ways of insulting their compatriots. BIFFO means 'Big Ignorant F--k-r From Offaly', Offaly being a not-very-glamorous Irish county. BUFFALO means 'Big Ugly F--k-r from Around Laois and Offaly'.

BRENDAN THE NAVIGATOR

A saintly Kerryman, which is an unusual enough combination. Brendan spent his early years being tended by angels, and as a young lad repelled an assault on his virtue by beating up a frisky little princess who tried to leap on his chariot. Having reviewed various career prospects, he settled on becoming a saint. He was advised to avoid scandal by not learning his saintly trade from a woman – a piece of advice which suggests that women were then among the prime authorities on monastic life. Finding none of the existing monastic rules to his taste, Brendan decided to write his own, or rather had them dictated to him by an angel. He was then ordained a priest.

One of Brendan's teachers had returned to Ireland from a sea voyage with the scent of paradise on his clothing, having stumbled across the Land of the Promise of Saints in his travels. Impressed by the odour, Brendan decided to set sail himself. He set off in his boat and put down at various islands, including one on which he found the body of a fair young woman, one hundred feet tall, who had been killed by a spear thrust. He restored her to life and baptised her, but had to give her the last sacraments and bury her when she died on him again. Brendan never had much luck with women. On another island he came across Judas Iscariot, being buffeted by the waves and struck constantly in the face by a flapping cloak. This struck him as rather a light penalty for having betrayed Christ, but Judas informed Brendan that this was not his punishment but his time off, since he was relieved of his torment on Sundays and major feast days. The story is somewhat reminiscent of the old joke about the new arrival who was being shown around hell, and was ushered into a room in which thousands of the damned were standing waist-deep in excrement, drinking cups of tea and chatting. The newcomer was just thinking to himself that this, though pretty unpleasant, was hardly as bad as he had feared, when a small devil dashed into the room shouting: 'Okay, tea break over, everybody back on their heads!'

Despite his fondness for water, Brendan cursed no less than fifty Irish rivers. As a penance he once crossed the sea to Britain, which for an Irishman would have been punishment enough. Readers may be distressed to hear that most of this is pure mythology. Even so, Brendan certainly existed, and probably built up a network of sea-linked monasteries in the sixth century. He might even have reached America, as its very first Irish immigrant. This has been shown to be physically possible: the skin-covered boats of the day were capable of making the crossing, and there were many tiny islands in the Atlantic occupied by holy men. Besides, the legends of Brendan's voyages reveal a good deal of knowledge of the Atlantic. The point of sea voyages for early Irish monks, however, wasn't to discover new continents, but to proclaim their faith in God by quite literally setting sail without a paddle. But they may always have bumped up against a few continents accidentally.

BRETHA CROLIGE

An early Irish legal document which refers to the three lawful wives a man may have – the principal wife, the concubine and the mistress – and justifies this polygamy by a pious appeal to the Old Testament. In early Ireland, polygamy was practised by the upper classes, and divorce and remarriage were common. In fact polygamy survived in some form until the end of the Middle Ages. Slavery existed in early Ireland too, and the Viking traders could be relied upon to provide the slaves – some of them prisoners of war, others children of the poor sold into slavery at times of famine. These provided a conveniently servile population to do the dirty work in the great monasteries, so that the monks themselves could be free to turn their minds to higher things, such as the ideals of human freedom and Christian compassion.

The legal unit of early Irish society was the family, not the individual. It was an intensely aristocratic, rank-conscious culture, with kings at the top and serfs at the bottom. The legal fine for kicking a bishop was considerably heavier than for kicking a peasant. The way to get on in life was to become the client of a rich lord, who would give you protection in return for military service. He would also give you a share of his plunder, along with some land and cows known as a fief. All he asked for in return was a sizeable share of your produce. For example, in return for a certain size of fief, you had to give your chief:

some free labour
one dairy cow
half the dripping of a year-old bull calf
a cauldron of new milk for cooking as sweet cheese with
    butter
a vessel of ripe cream
twenty loaves of bread
a slab of butter eight inches wide and four inches thick
two fistfuls of Welsh onions and two Welsh leeks
a flitch of bacon 36 inches long
another calf.

The lord was also entitled to one night's partying at his client's house, which given the amount he tended to guzzle could prove a ruinous affair. Some historians consider that the client would have been a lot better off just committing suicide.

Actually, there was no need to kill yourself, since disease was very likely to do it for you. Major epidemics of what were probably dysentery, influenzal pneumonia, plague, smallpox, rabies and famine fever struck every generation from the seventh to the ninth centuries. The only cure was prayer and applying saintly relics to yourself. Surprisingly for such a religious people, these didn't always work.

CELTIC TIGER

Sometimes 'Emerald Tiger', a phrase used to describe Ireland's currently booming economy. After decades of stagnation and protectionism, the Irish opened up their economy in the 1960s, and joined the European Community in 1973. They have had mixed economic fortunes since:

overall, Ireland's rate of growth of national income this century may well have been the worst in western Europe. But these days the Irish are riding the highest tidal wave of prosperity they have ever known. Of course, by the time you read this, they may have been plunged into recession again. But in some economic respects Ireland has now even overtaken its old sparring-partner Britain. In 1996, for the first time in its history, the country produced more wealth per head of population than Britain did. In 1998, the largest Irish banking group reported profits of more than £800 million. In 1995, Irish consumers spent £22 billion pounds on goods and services. Ireland now has more owners of video games than any other nation in the world, thus ruining the country's visual sense even further. It's now also one place ahead of the United Kingdom in the international league table of economic competitiveness, which makes it the eleventh most competitive nation in the world. Some economists regard this measurement as largely meaningless.

Even so, Ireland still qualifies for huge financial handouts from Europe (about £1.2 billion a year), and has traditionally been counted as one of the European Union's three poorest countries (the other two are Greece and Portugal). This aid, however, is now about to be cut by 80% over the next few years. Success has its liabilities. Up to the 1960s, Ireland had many of the features of a Third World country. Most of these have vanished, but some traces still remain, not least in Irish habits of mind. As someone remarked, Ireland is a First World country with a Third World memory. It's also a nation with high economic expectations and a lack of resources to meet them fully.

Quite what world Ireland belongs to, First or Third, has been the subject of some fierce debate. Indeed there is little in Ireland that isn't fiercely debated. Until about the 1960s,

Ireland could well have been loosely described as a Third World country. Nowadays it's lodged firmly within the so-called First World, somewhere in the league table of richest nations. But how prosperous a country may be isn't the only measure of its world status. Despite its relative affluence, Ireland still betrays a lot of symptoms of classic underdevelopment. It's still a lopsided economy, heavily reliant on foreign capital, and with a weak industrial base of its own. The British never significantly industrialised the place; in fact much of Ireland was steadily *de*-industrialised throughout the nineteenth century. Like some Third World nations, it has a political system which partly depends on favours, tribal affinities and who you happen to prop up the bar with. Many of its legal and political institutions are hangovers from the days of colonial rule. Like some underdeveloped countries too, it's culturally dependent on more advanced countries, living in the shadow of Britain and the States despite its own robust cultural traditions. Its TV network, for example, imports a huge amount of foreign material. Some of its mentality is still deeply traditionalist, though this is everywhere eroding. And it's a migrant society, which until quite recently has been unable, like Turkey or the Caribbean, to provide enough employment at home for its own people. It would be foolish to categorise Ireland with Nigeria and Nepal; but though it clearly isn't a Third World country, some of it has a one-and-a half world feel about it.

In one sense, the old Ireland lingers on. It's still, geographically, an overwhelmingly rural society, with a host of small towns and a mere handful of major settlements. Over 80% of the land is under agricultural cultivation, and Dublin is deeply untypical of the country as a whole. Some of the more sophisticated Irish speak of 'rural Ireland', as though this were a specific sector of the country rather like the Lake District in England. This is misleading: Ireland *is* mostly rural, which means among other things that 'rural Ireland' is a varied, complex place, not some kind of monolith. Tipperary is vastly different from Donegal. Some of the more modern-minded Irish like to persuade themselves that rural Ireland has actually disappeared, which may come as a surprise to some Kerry farmers. They mean that it's been transformed, but so has urban Ireland, so on this logic that's disappeared too. It's true, though, that consumerism, tourism, mass media, new industry and travel have all conspired to narrow the gap between rural and urban.

Despite this, agriculture was for a long time the biggest Irish industry, though these days it employs directly only a small fraction of the population, around 11%. However, if you throw in all those indirectly involved in the industry, it pans out at a much higher percentage – near to one quarter of the working population. A sizeable amount of agricultural production is exported. Ireland's other major export is itself. All those jokey postcards and sentimental tea-towels are part of the way the country faithfully panders to the tourist's starry-eyed image of it, without actually believing it in the least. Irishness is the intoxicating liquor which the country is best at distilling. Consumed too freely, it produces more fantasies, hallucinations, false hopes, weepiness, bravado and phoney cheeriness than Bushmills ever did. The country is well on the way to becoming one enormous theme park, a kind of Celtic Disneyland with Queen Maeve standing in for Mickey Mouse.

Foreign capital has poured into Ireland over recent decades, given few financial restrictions, the lowest corporate tax for manufacturers in Europe and good industrial relations. Polls suggest that the Irish are more hostile to unofficial strikes and protest movements than other European nations. It also helps that they speak English, and have an attractive country for foreigners to settle in. Ireland today is a world leader in such areas as chemicals and electronics. But some 35-40% of Irish industry is foreign-owned, and foreign firms account for a huge percentage of manufactured exports. At a highly conservative estimate, around £1 billion in profits flows out of the country each year. Little of this profit is reinvested in Ireland, and there's a notable lack of sizeable native industry. The Irish have fallen over themselves to attract the transnational corporations, offering subsidies and tax inducements and waiving a lot of restrictions. The positive result has been affluence for some; the negative result is that the country, having been for centuries a floating off-shore farm for Britain, is now in danger of becoming an off-shore tax haven for US big business.

So this precarious prosperity is deeply dependent on outside sources. Much of it comes down to a few US-owned high-tech industries. It hasn't touched the country's growing number of poor, and high-income households in the country are still very much in the minority. In one survey, two-thirds of the Irish felt that they weren't profiting personally from the boom. Unemployment has run at up to 21% over the last decade, a heavy burden of social security on a not-very-affluent state.[6] (Another such burden is education, given that having children is one of Ireland's major industries.)[7] The

---

[6] FIF: Around 35% of the Irish are dependent on social welfare.
[7] FIF: Dublin has the oldest maternity hospital in Europe, the Rotunda, which is an excellent name for a maternity hospital. The country is famed for its obstetrical skills, and doctors in this branch of the business flock to it from overseas.

country had for a long time the highest unemployment rate in the industrialised world, along with Spain; in some run-down urban areas it can hit 70% or higher. Around one million people are estimated to live on or below the poverty line, including one third of all Irish children. Next to the USA, Ireland has the highest percentage of low-paid workers in the developed world.

Like most other developed societies, Ireland now has a disaffected underclass of the long-term unemployed, concentrated in urban ghettoes whose very names send a chill down the spines of more well-heeled citizens. A recent study suggests that the country's run-down public housing estates have the lowest allocation in Europe of resources such as education, shopping, leisure and childcare. One such estate in Dublin has one shop to serve 15,000 inhabitants; another estate of over 5,000 people has no school, doctor's surgery, phone box or mail box. On the other hand, Irish public housing estates also have the highest proportion of self-help groups in Europe.

When economic recession hits Europe in general, one traditional solution to Irish unemployment – emigration – is no longer available, so the ranks of the jobless are swollen even more. There has been a mass exodus from decaying rural areas into deprived urban ones. Only about one third of Irish farms are viable as full-time operations, and the country has few mineral resources to compensate. The Irish are paid lower salaries than the British, but on the whole are taxed more highly, and the cost of living is about 20% higher than in the neighbouring island. Those tourists expecting Ireland to be cheap are in for a rude shock; one evening in the pub could clean you out for a fortnight.

After centuries of grinding poverty, the Irish deserve a break. Luxuries, or even in some cases necessities, which they only dreamed of, can now be theirs. But as always, there's a price to pay. The country is becoming more cynical, more greedy and scandal-ridden, more sharply polarised between the business millionaires, who in Ireland have something like the status of pop stars, and the dismal ranks of the unemployed. The Celtic tiger is certainly roaring, but tigers in Ireland are confined to very small areas known as zoos. Like economic booms, they don't cover the whole country.

For a long time, confessing that you were Irish was like announcing that you were a cross between a clown and a mental defective. Now, in the 1990s, it's as cool to be Irish as it was to hail from Merseyside in the 1960s. It involves just the right balance of being centre-stage and slightly off-beat, exotic yet reassuringly normal. As the Irish have grown more self-assured at home, they have created bigger waves abroad; but the process has also worked in reverse. The more 'mainstream' or 'on-line' the country becomes in cosmopolitan terms, the more it feels confident to explore its own distinctive cultural identity. The more it comes to look like everyone else, the more, oddly, it can feel free to be itself. In one sense this isn't surprising, in a world where distinctive cultural identities have become commodities on the global market. In another sense, it's remarkable how these two aspects of Irishness have worked to reinforce each other. It's exactly the opposite of the old colonial situation, where the Irish could never quite be themselves because they were too busy trying to make themselves acceptable to others. Those who fall over themselves to become insiders simply betray what outsiders they really are, as the doomed career of the Dubliner Oscar Wilde well illustrates. The Irish no longer feel that they have to assert themselves so much. The trouble with having to affirm your identity, necessary though it may sometimes be, is that it's hard to enjoy it.

Part of what makes Ireland distinctive is a history of hunger, backwardness and political dependency. It's this which has so often driven it in upon itself; but it's also what might now help to open it up. Because of their troubled history, the Irish ought to have some sympathy for other small, struggling nations around the world. Whether the country will take this political path, or whether it will just end up as another Switzerland, still remains to be seen.

CELTS

Nobody knows exactly when the Celts came to Ireland, but it was most likely a protracted process which took place during the last few centuries BC. Some of them probably arrived in the country from Roman Britain, while others probably came directly from the Continent. The Celts hailed originally from a region north of the Alps, but were soon to be found everywhere from the Danube basin in central Europe to Spain and Asia Minor. Some scholars have detected Eastern influences, including Indian ones, in early Irish culture. It seems that the ancient Celts of Britain and Ireland didn't call themselves Celts, in rather the same way as nobody would call themselves Fatso. It was a name which came to be used of them sometime in the eighteenth century.

After the Greeks and the Romans, the Celts were the most significant European culture of the early Middle Ages. Next to Latin, Irish is the European language with the longest, best-documented development. Only in Ireland did there survive a language and literature which could claim direct descent from the ancient Celts, untainted by the Roman empire.

The Celts hit their stride in the fifth and fourth centuries BC. They sacked Rome, and are said to have charged into battle stark naked, perhaps hoping to give their enemies a quick jab in the guts while their eyes were modestly closed. They were said by some to be addicted to alcohol, poetry and fighting, while others have seen them as the brilliant failures of the ancient world, a people who overran vast kingdoms but couldn't finish what they started. They were finally beaten back by the Romans and driven to the margins of Europe. To the Romans they were noble savages, as they were for some of the British later. Quarrelsome and unruly, plunged into perpetual warfare, they were unable to make common cause against an enemy. The Celts were dab hands at culture and cattle raiding, but not so adept at political cohesion.

CHILDREN

The Irish have sometimes been patronised as children – ironically, since Irish children are on the whole impressively mature. They are less coy and cute than Anglo-Saxon kids, less conscious of themselves as a race apart. In general, they're sensible without being revoltingly precocious. This may have to do with the culture of a rural society, where children must traditionally work alongside their elders; it may also be connected with the fact that sentimentality was a luxury the Irish could ill-afford. (They are similarly unsentimental about animals, another rural characteristic, unlike the urbanised English for whom animals are primarily pets.)

It may also have to do with the fact that Irish children are likely to have quite a few siblings, and so have to share some parental responsibility and can't hog the limelight so much. Less benignly, it may be the result of a nation where authoritarian attitudes have been fairly common, and where children are thus granted less leeway to indulge themselves. Older children in Ireland also have to bear a lot of pressure, and the suicide rate among children and adolescents has been steadily rising. The school Leaving Certificate has become a kind of national mania, with help lines, private tuition, professional counselling and a number of near-nervous breakdowns. Whatever the explanation, Irish children don't need to be talked down to and can usually hold their own in adult company, without feeling the need to grab attention by parades of pure silliness. As the old saying goes, children may be obscene but not absurd ...

COMPUTERS

These are a cunning device used by the Irish in order to get back to their old, easy rhythm of life. Have you noticed what happens these days, in Ireland or anywhere else, when you try to check into a hotel or buy an air ticket? The guy behind the desk spends fifteen minutes tapping away at his machine. He is obviously writing a book in his spare time, and has decided to add another chapter while you wait. The point of computers is to escape from the speed and bustle of modern life, where the hotel clerk (as used to happen) just seizes a book and slaps your name down in five seconds. Computers are part of a conspiracy to return us to the leisurely pace of pre-technological days. That's why you'll find so many of them in Ireland.

CRAIC

(Pronounced 'crack', and not to be confused with a form of cocaine): Irish for 'fun', 'having a good time', usually a mixture of music, drink and talk. An over-used term, now rapidly approaching the status of 'begorrah'. Is Irish *craic* a myth? You must be joking. Few nations on earth know how to enjoy themselves like the Irish. This is partly because, unlike Anglo-Saxon types, they have little history of Puritanism. (The Protestant North is a different matter, here as in most other things.) The Irish are guilt-free in more or less everything but sex, about which they have been as repressive and benighted as most other nations. The younger generation, however, is changing all that; and even the sexual hang-ups of their elders, much fuelled by Roman Catholicism, are arguably a recent historical development.

Traditional Gaelic culture was bawdy, explicit, sometimes downright obscene. But once the Irish realised that too many children was economically unwise, they began to police their sexuality and control their fertility. In fact by the end of the last century they had more unmarried persons, and more late marriages for those who took the plunge, than any other European nation. Thirty per cent of Irish men and 23% of Irish women never married. The Irishman who thinks that the age of fifty might be a bit early to get hitched hasn't completely vanished.

Sex aside, however – and that was the unhappy situation of many of them – the Irish are by and large a less inhibited, more gregarious bunch than the Anglo-Saxons. (Though like most things in Ireland, this isn't the whole truth: the Irish are also thought to have a brooding, melancholic streak, as some of their exquisitely sorrowful music would suggest. Maybe this is a hangover from a grim, famine-ridden past.) The

English consider it permissible to use each other's Christian names after, say, the eighth meeting, and even then squirm with embarrassment, as though they have accidentally let rip a rude sound. The Irish, like the Americans, use first names straight off, and on meeting always ask after each others' health, which the English hardly ever do. The English would let you die in squalor and solitude simply because they were afraid of invading your privacy. Despite all this, Irish culture is also devious, complex and multi-layered. It's very much an in-group culture, full of codes, hints and signals which an outsider has to decipher. Beneath the appearance of openness, Irish society is a fairly guarded place, a lot less accessible than it seems, with a notable gap between public appearance and private reality. It's an intimate society, but also an incestuous one. The Irish, even in the posher suburbs of Dublin, are a lot more clannish and neighbourly than their British neighbours, as well as gossipy, back-biting and endlessly inquisitive. You might look out of your window one morning to find a neighbour mowing your lawn. If this happened to you in Canterbury or Chicago, you'd probably call the police. But your neighbours will also know your business better than you do. Someone once observed that Dublin had marvellous acoustics, meaning that if you whisper in one corner of the city you can hear it in another.

This may be a hangover from the old rural Ireland, where life was more tribal and claustrophobic than it is in Cheltenham or California. It also springs from the fact that it's a very small country, where no point is more than seventy miles from the sea, and where everyone seems to know everyone else. You can be sure that the brother-in-law of your hairdresser lives two doors away from a second cousin of your cosmetic surgeon. If you want the telephone company to repair your phone, you don't ring them up, since chances are they won't reply (Irish telephone companies don't seem to have telephones), and even if they do it might take them months to get round to it (see EASY-GOINGNESS). Instead, you talk to that feller with the cast in his left eye you keep bumping into in the supermarket, who someone has told you is the brother of a woman who goes out with a clerk in Telecom Eireann. The phone will be repaired within the week.

An Irish joke will illustrate the point. Three candidates are being interviewed for the post of government statistician. Each is asked to add three to four. The first comes up with six, the second with five, the third with seven. Which one got the job? Why, the one who was the cousin of the Minister, stupid.

Though the most important activity in Ireland today is making money, the Irish are still less obsessive about the business than their Anglo-Saxon counterparts. Whereas British telephone directories list businesses first and private numbers second, in Ireland it's the other way round. A country which traditionally lacked a spirit of commercial enterprise is still rather sceptical about getting on in life. If you're buying an article in a shop and find yourself a few pence short of the price, they will probably let you off the extra change. It wouldn't happen in New York. I remember the amazement with which an American friend greeted the news that Irish builders traditionally lay coins in the foundations of new houses for good luck. He couldn't have been more flabbergasted if I'd told him that they slaughtered a new-born baby and buried it under the floorboards.

CUISINE

Irish cuisine is a bit of a myth, even though some restaurants now peddle it. Basically, it means fancy ways of serving up fish and potatoes.[8] Irish stew isn't Irish. Few of the Irish were rich enough to afford meat and vegetables. It was invented for Irish workers in Britain. Irish coffee is Irish, but these days, like leprechauns and the Book of Kells, it's mainly for the tourists.[9] You can find lots of restaurants in Ireland these days which rival Parisian ones in their culinary expertise, but otherwise Ireland's main contribution to cosmopolitan cooking is deep fried lard, in which they dip more or less everything except their toe-nails (and even that's not certain). Traditional Irish fare was rather more simple.

For breakfast you had a helping of potatoes. Then, for lunch, you ate a dish of spuds. For dinner, just by way of a change, you chewed on a few praties, the Irish word for (you guessed it) potatoes. If you were lucky you had a bit of buttermilk to wash them down, and if you lived near enough to the coast there was always fish, though the Irish were too poor to have a full-scale fishing industry. This is why, when the potato crop failed in the 1840s, millions of Irish perished or emigrated, since they had nothing else to eat. They grew crops, but they had to sell these to pay the landlord his rent. A few decades later, half the population had disappeared.

There are, even so, certain dishes which claim to be traditionally Irish. You could try *boxty*, for example, which is really an upmarket version of potato cake. Alternatively, there's carrageen moss blancmange. The bad news is that it

---

[8] FIF: Ireland now imports most of its potatoes.
[9] FIF: Irish coffee was invented by a chef at Shannon airport to defrost transatlantic pilots in the early days of air travel.

really is made out of moss, mixed with milk, sugar and lemon rind. If you're partial to sheep's blood, you can always sample *drisheen*, which contains a couple of pints of the stuff. Half a pint of pig's blood and a handful of intestines, on the other hand, will make you a fine black pudding to start off the day. Then there's grunt soup, which is easy to make if you can find out what a grunt is. Several have starved in the process. For pig's head brawn, remember to scrape the pig's head free of eyes, brains and gristle, as well as giving the pig's feet a good scrub. If you pickle the feet, you get something called crubeens. If none of this appeals to you, you can just throw a sod of grass into boiling water and hope for the best.

The Irish eat too much, on average exceeding the recommended daily calorie intake by over 60%. They also

eat unhealthily: not much fresh fruit, cabbage rather than salad, meat rather than fish (despite swarms of them offshore). They consume only about half as much fish as the Spanish do, but knock back a frightening amount of dairy produce, just as they did in ancient times. They have a rabid passion for sweet stuff, and are still Europe's premier potato eaters. An orally fixated nation, they lavish an astounding 16% of their expenditure on beverages and tobacco, an amount five times that of Spain and eight times that of Luxembourg.

The most easily prepared traditional Irish food of all is known as potato and point. Irish peasants liked their potatoes with a bit of salt, but if there was no salt available, they just pointed their potato at the dish in the middle of the table where it was supposed to be. When it comes to traditional Irish food, imagining that you're eating the stuff is sometimes preferable to the real thing.

DEAFNESS

A curiously common Irish affliction, especially among middle-aged men. Eavesdrop on a conversation between them, and you'll notice that every few minutes one or both will say 'ah?' a sound somewhere between a grunt and a snarl. Sometimes they say 'ah?' even before the other person has said enough for there to be anything to mishear. This has nothing to do with the state of Irish ears, and everything to do with an annoying habit of not attending to the other person. Especially if she's your wife. There's even an Irish speech habit in which you pass a comment and then tack 'What?' on to the end of it, as though you haven't heard what you've just said.

The deafest people in Ireland are the armed forces. An astonishingly high proportion of them are hard of hearing as a result of their professional activities. This may have something to do with a successful law suit for damages brought by one soldier, which then escalated into an avalanche of law suits which in theory could cost the Irish state over £5 billion. Who said that the phrase 'military intelligence' was a contradiction in terms?

DEBAUCHERY

There is no debauchery in Ireland, as the Church would not allow it. You must be thinking of ...

DEBUNKERY

... of which there's a great amount. The Irish are superlative mockers, not least of themselves. They are allergic to pomp and pretentiousness, and love nothing more than cutting them satirically down to size. It's a strikingly informal culture, without much ceremony or mystique: the old guy with the pock-marked nose drinking on the other side of the bar really could be the Prime Minister. He may have one or two minders hanging about, but certainly not a posse of armed secret service agents. Well-known public figures who in Britain or the USA wouldn't dream of being listed in the telephone directory can be found there in Ireland. It's a reasonably egalitarian society, although as with most other places the gap between rich and poor is steadily widening. As someone once observed, the Americans have no class structure, the British have nothing but a class structure, and the Irish have a class structure but nobody's yet discovered what it is.

The Irish dislike solemn rhetoric and self-display. If an American tells them that he has some Truly Wonderful Children, they will delight in informing him that their own kids are junkies and jailbirds, even if they're actually research physicists. Irish humour is perverse, dark-edged and latently aggressive, in contrast to the wisecracking of the States or the bland heartiness of some Brits. A lot of Irish speech is aimed at deflating rather than affirming. Few nations have such a keen sense of the ridiculous, not least when it comes to themselves. Ireland has a dynamic economy but not a dynamic mentality.

Boasting and exaggeration are traditional Irish habits, partly as a way of bulling yourself up when others have been doing you down. It was also the duty of the bards of early

Irish society to lavish absurdly extravagant praise on their chiefs, which is one possible source of the Irish talent for hyperbole. But boasting was also frowned on in a traditionally poverty-stricken culture where one person's gain was likely to be another's loss, and where everyone knows you too well anyway to be fooled. So Irish conversation often plays down achievement. You didn't have a five-course banquet last night, you had a bit of a nibble. This can be taken to ludicrous limits. A medical friend tells me of an interview he had with a patient. Had he had any serious illnesses? No, no, none at all. Was he sure? Well, he had a 'touch of cancer' a while back.

In this, the Irish resemble the English, who are similarly low-keyed and self-effacing. But whereas the English are a nation of masochistic moaners who love nothing better than a good grouse (in fact God created their frightful weather for just that reason), the Irish are ironic about themselves without being whiners. They love doing themselves down; it's just when *you* try to do it that they get all prickly, with the touchiness of a people used to being sneered at. The Irish may tell you how disgusted they are by the corruption of the Catholic Church, or by sentimental talk of the Emerald Isle. But if you, as an outsider, join in and criticise the place too, they'll suddenly get a lot more patriotic than they were ten minutes ago.

DESPARD, CHARLOTTE

Born of a famous French family, Charlotte Despard grew up in late nineteenth century London, and became known as the 'Mother of Battersea' for her work among the London poor. She joined the Independent Labour Party and was later a member of the British Communist Party. As honorary secretary of the suffragette Women's Social and Political Union, she saw the inside of a prison more than once. A pacifist as well as a feminist, she was a prominent figure in the campaign against the First World War, and was also an early worker for animals' rights. Her love of horses remained heroically unaffected by the experience of being charged by mounted police in Trafalgar Square.

Always eager to seek out new comrades, Despard established spiritualist contact with the Italian nationalist leader Mazzini, who didn't allow the fact that he was dead to interfere with their conversations. She also established a teetotal pub in London called the Despard Arms, which sounds rather like opening a vegetarian butcher's shop. At the age of 77, restless for new horizons, she widened her sphere of activity by moving to Ireland, where she teamed up with Maud Gonne (see GONNE) in the women's defence league for republican prisoners. ('Maud Gone Mad and Charlotte Desperate', as they were irreverently known.) She also threw in her lot with the Irish Vegetarian Society, whose president was a Mrs Ham and whose vice-presidents were Mrs Hogg and Mrs Joynt.

Active in the ranks of those who opposed the partition of Ireland, Despard opened a jam factory for the unemployed and joined the Irish Workers' Party. She soon found herself branded as a dangerously subversive type by the Irish government, ripe for deportation because of her non-Irish nationality. Among her other major achievements, she was cordially detested by the poet William Yeats. In 1932 she travelled to the Soviet Union, a land for which she displayed a naively uncritical admiration. She also founded a workers' college in Dublin, which was sacked by an angry mob.

At the age of 90, half-blind, rheumatic and arthritic, Charlotte Despard moved to Northern Ireland to continue her work in Belfast. When the Spanish Civil War broke out in the 1930s she insisted on visiting Spain to join in, but was persuaded to content herself with speaking against Spanish fascism at international rallies. She died a bankrupt, no doubt wondering which country she should conquer next.

DOLMENS

One of the many types of ancient stones you can find in Ireland. They usually consist of a capstone supported by a number of upright slabs or boulders. The country is also littered with between 30,000 and 40,000 ancient forts, sometimes known as *raths*, which are mostly circular rings of earth surrounded by a ditch, sometimes with elaborate underground caves with traps and trick passageways. They were probably used not as military bases, but as homesteads and cattle enclosures. You'll also find tumili (ancient burial mounds), cairns (piles of loose stones) and crannogs, which are artificial islands built in lakes. *Gallans* are pillar or standing stones, sometimes ornamented, which occur either singly or in lines. Some of them are inscribed with the oldest form of writing known in Ireland, Ogham, which consists of a simple system of cut lines.

Irish scholars have now discarded the theory that some of these burial places were also ancient bus shelters. Combining the two, however, wouldn't be a bad idea in the Ireland of today. An alarming proportion of the Irish population has been known to die while waiting for buses, of grief, frustration, exposure, or just natural ageing.

DRACULA

Not everybody knows that Dracula was Irish. He came from
Dublin, not from Transylvania. The original Dracula novel
was the work of the Dublin writer Bram Stoker, a civil
servant turned theatrical manager. The Irish have produced a
number of monsters and bloodsuckers in their time, but this
one is the best known. It is a slur on the Irish people that
Dracula's habit of sleeping during the day and roaming
around at night is modelled on those of them who can't get
out of bed in the morning.

DRIVING

Driving is a barbarous Irish custom, at least in the capital. Not having been to war for ages, the Irish have taken instead to massacring each other on the highways. The road death toll is fast becoming one of the worst in Europe, and proportionately speaking the Irish die on the roads at twice the rate the British do. It's dangerous to take the rules too seriously, since not enough other drivers do. By breaking them systematically, you might just get yourself from one end of a city to another, though there's no guarantee of it. Dublin drivers are notably impatient and discourteous. Like the British, the Irish drive on the left, though sometimes it's hard to tell. If they ever change over to driving on the right, they will probably do so gradually, since most things in the country take time. First the buses, then the trucks, then the private cars. It couldn't result in more slaughter than there is now.

One of the hazards of Irish modernisation is that Dublin, a small colonial capital with fairly narrow streets, has now swollen almost to bursting point, as thousands of new cars flood into a ramshackle, badly planned road network each year. Over 145,000 new cars were registered in 1998. In fact planning and conservation in Dublin have been grievously neglected, throwing the place open to some ruthless property development. If some of the Irish had their way, they would tear down Dublin Castle and replace it with a car park. Dublin has some noble eighteenth-century buildings and some hideous modern ones. The Irish have little tradition of civic responsibility. In colonial times, they passed this buck to their British rulers, and have grown used to seeing themselves as passive consumers rather than as active citizens.

The county is an extraordinary jumble of the sublime and the shabby. Not long ago, if you wanted to build a fifteen-floor hotel in your front garden, you probably wouldn't bother applying for planning permission, you'd just go ahead and do it. The countryside is littered with ugly-looking bungalows (one-floor houses). There's not much atmospheric pollution, but that's because there's not much industry. Buses in Ireland tend to arrive according to some astrological calendar unknown to the rest of us. There are parking laws, but like a lot of other laws in the country they're not taken too seriously (see EASY-GOINGNESS). As an excruciating old Irish joke has it, a single yellow line by the side of the road means you can't park at all, while a double yellow line means you can't park at all at all. However, rather late in the day, the Irish are now becoming more aware of their environment. Previously they thought it was a figment of the imagination, like fairies and pink elephants; nowadays they are starting to clean up the mess, not least because otherwise they may scare off the tourists. Though the tourists are starting to pose an environmental hazard too ...

DUBLIN 4

Some people think that the Loch Ness monster is a myth, though the Loch Ness monster itself presumably wouldn't agree. With Dublin 4, it's the other way round: the people who live there tend to think it's a myth, whereas a lot of people who don't live there think it's real. Dublin 4 is less an actual area (though there is a Dublin postal district of that number), than a phrase used to refer to a certain intellectual elite in the city. This includes writers, broadcasters, journalists and the liberal-minded, professional middle classes in general.

To be a fully paid-up member of Dublin 4 you have to eat polenta, send your children to fee-paying schools, have a superior attitude to rural Ireland, criticise the Catholic Church and the traditional political set-up, take holidays in Tuscany or Provence, own a cottage in the west of Ireland, think nationalism frightfully old-hat, and regard Mary Robinson, the progressive-minded former President of Ireland, as a divine creature a cut or two above the Virgin Mary. To belong to Dublin 4, you also have to regard the whole existence of Dublin 4 as a myth dreamt up by the resentful masses who eat bacon and cabbage rather than polenta, send their children to state schools, can't afford to take a holiday, and when asked 'Have you read Marx?' reply 'Only where I sit down'.

Some denizens of Dublin 4 tend to see themselves as liberal-minded and the rest of the Irish as sunk in redneck opinions and rural idiocy. This is almost certainly a myth. Opinion polls suggest that on many issues the Irish are no more conservative than other Europeans. They're as liberal as other Europeans on the question of working or single mothers, and are coming slowly into line with them on sexual freedom for the unmarried. They're more likely than the rest of Europe to believe that both work and family are very important, and they place a very high value on marital fidelity. As with many people today, their values are typically a mixture of modern and traditional. Where they *are* more conservative than their European counterparts is on questions of authority. On the whole, the Irish are more likely to be respectful of authority than, say, the French or the Italians. Irish Catholicism is an obvious influence here, or even, further back in history, the deference paid to the chief. The Irish are generally less inclined than other European countries to give a high priority to freedom of speech. In fact they've devoted a considerable amount of energy to trying to kill it off (see X-RATED).

DUN LAOGHAIRE

(Pronounced 'Dunleary'.) The place just south of Dublin where you get the boat to England. In 1821, King George IV landed near here to inspect his loyal Irish subjects. He was said to be 'speechless' as he staggered off the boat, and there was a loyal Irish suspicion that this was not because of the sublimity of the Irish landscape. He then shot off on a flying visit to his mistress, but cancelled his scheduled tour of the country. This was a great disappointment to those notables who had spent six months rebuilding their country mansions in order to receive him in style, but perhaps not quite so crushing a disappointment to the plain people of Ireland. The official reason for the cancellation was the death of his wife, though some of the more cynical Irish suspected that it was because he was too inebriated to put one foot in front of the other. On his way back home, still shaky on his pins, he did the Irish people the great honour of allowing Dun Laoghaire to be renamed 'Kingstown', after himself. At the first opportunity, however, the ungrateful Irish re-renamed it Dun Laoghaire, largely because the British don't know how to pronounce it.

EASTER 1916

A date as engraved on Irish memory as Independence Day in the States or Remembrance Sunday in Britain. It was the Easter Monday on which a group of nationalist revolutionaries took over the General Post Office in Dublin's O'Connell Street, and held the city for several days against the firepower of the British army. The insurrection was to lead indirectly, five years later, to Irish political independence.

Like a lot of uprisings, this one was something of a muddle. As one Irish writer remarked: 'The birth of a nation is never an Immaculate Conception'. The insurrection was planned for Easter Sunday, for symbolic reasons, but happened a day late. The rebels themselves were mostly poets and intellectuals, rarely the most promising material for a military scrap. One of them used to carry a swordstick and wear a cloak; another wore a kilt and played the bagpipes in the lulls between the fighting. (Perhaps nobody had told him that the kilt was a foreign importation into Ireland.) Another of the rebel leaders sported Celtic rings and bracelets, and got married in prison in a midnight ceremony on the eve of his execution. Despite the theatricality, they were courageous patriots who were prepared to lay down their lives for political freedom.

The Rising was led by Patrick Pearse, son of an English stonemason whose statues you can see adorning the roof of the Bank of Ireland in College Green. What is now Pearse Street in Dublin is where he had his workshop. Pearse Junior led a small band of his volunteers up O'Connell Street, apparently on routine manoeuvres, then suddenly wheeled and stormed the Post Office. The desk clerks soon realised that they hadn't come in to buy postage stamps. Pearse then read out the celebrated proclamation of the Provisional Government from the steps of the Post Office, just to let the bemused public know that this wasn't a piece of street theatre. (In fact, the press which printed the proclamation was installed in the Abbey Theatre, and the first man to die in the uprising was an Abbey actor.) The rebels then dashed around the city to stick up copies of the proclamation, but discovered that they had forgotten the paste.

Meanwhile, other key posts throughout Dublin were commandeered. One of them was Jacob's biscuit factory, rather an inglorious venue for a revolution, where the poet and university lecturer Thomas MacDonagh was in command. One of his senior officers was John MacBride, a bone-headed drunk who once gave a speech in Paris in such bad French that the audience thought that he was speaking Dutch. MacBride just happened to be in Dublin attending a wedding, noticed that there was an insurrection afoot and cheerfully joined in. He was to be executed later for his affability. Other buildings occupied were a flour mill which was under the command of the man later to become leader of the Irish Free State, the mathematician Eamon de Valera.

De Valera had been born in New York, a fortunate accident which was to save him from a death sentence.

The British army, caught badly off-guard, soon reacted to the Rising, and fighting raged in the capital for about a week. Most of the citizens still went calmly about their business: the *Irish Times* carried on being published, and there was tea at the Shelbourne Hotel every day, just as there is today. Some of the plain people of Dublin played their patriotic part in undermining the British economy by looting shops in O'Connell Street, where small urchins could be seen staggering off with boxes of chocolates. Some of their elders could be observed leisurely trying on shoes and jewellery in shop windows, or even stripping off entirely to try on a suit of clothes. A British gunboat entered the River Liffey and began shelling the agitators. The dashing Constance Markievicz (see MARKIEVICZ), a great favourite with the Dublin poor, commanded a squad of rebels who dug trenches in St Stephen's Green. This was literally short-sighted, since the Green was overlooked by tall buildings from which the British could easily fire on them.

The Rising was meant to be an all-Ireland affair, but though there was some military action in Galway and elsewhere, the country as a whole failed to rise up. This was partly because members of the Irish Republican Brotherhood, the outfit which spearheaded the uprising and is the forerunner of today's IRA, were thrown into confusion by a series of coded messages first declaring the rebellion on, then calling it off. Things weren't helped either by the failure of a plan to land German arms for the rebels on the Irish coast (Britain was at war with Germany at the time). Roger Casement, the officer in charge of the shipment, stepped ashore out of a German submarine only to be instantly arrested. He too was later to be executed by the British.

An Irish nurse tending the wounded in O'Connell Street was later rewarded by the British with a part in a West End review called *Three Cheers*. Fires spread quickly throughout the capital, and there was some fierce house-to-house fighting. The general in command of the British troops later more or less acknowledged that some of his men had committed atrocities. There was some indiscriminate murder of innocent civilians by British soldiers. One British officer later commented: 'The Irish ought to be grateful to us. With a minimum of casualties to the civilian population, we have succeeded in removing some third-rate poets'. As the roof of the Post Office gradually collapsed, the rebels evacuated their stronghold, and finally decided to surrender in order to prevent more civilian casualties. A rebel soldier was sent out with a white flag, whom the British promptly shot. Finally a young Irish nurse tried her luck in a hail of bullets, and was received by the British Commandant. The Rising left some hundreds of dead, and around £2.5 million worth of damage. O'Connell Street was in ruins, and as the dispirited rebels were led away they were jeered by some of the fellow citizens for whom they had fought. When informed that there had been an insurrection in Dublin, the English Prime Minister said, 'Well, that's really something', and went to bed.

It was then that the British turned their own victory into defeat by shooting the leaders of the revolt. One of them, the labour leader James Connolly, had been wounded in the foot in the Post Office and had to be executed sitting in a chair. As sixteen of the rebels were killed in batches, the mood of the Irish people turned to fury. Some of them prayed for their dead heroes, while some even prayed *to* them. A few years later, the nationalist party Sinn Fein (which, ironically, had had nothing to do with the Rising) swept the board at a general election and decided to declare their own government. The result was war between Ireland and Britain, which ended in 1921 with the Treaty and the birth the following year of the Irish Free State. At least one famous Irishman, Oscar Wilde, would have disagreed with this settlement had he lived to see it; he believed that Ireland should rule Britain.

In some respects, the Easter Rising remains a puzzling affair. Did the nationalists really think that they could take on the might of the British army, or was their action intended as a symbolic 'blood sacrifice' which might stir their compatriots to revolt? Were they militants or martyrs? Might they have stood some chance of victory if their original plan had not collapsed? Was the Rising completely unnecessary? Britain had in fact already promised Home Rule to the Irish, but had shelved the measure for the duration of the First World War. Was it an act of heroism or one of treachery – a stab in the back for those Irishmen who were fighting alongside Britain in the First World War?

Like a lot of events in Irish history, the Rising today is the subject of some ferocious controversy. These days, the Irish government is notably reluctant to celebrate the anniversary of the event, for fear that it might give comfort to the IRA. The last real commemoration was in 1966, when the Rising was marked among other things by the building of a hideous set of working-class apartment blocks on the edge of Dublin, which the Irish have been listlessly trying to tear down ever since. Critics of Irish nationalism tend to see the insurrection as the madcap adventurism of a bunch of Romantic idealists; its defenders point to the fact that it was a relatively unbloody affair, and that it did after all lead indirectly to political independence. The British might have honoured their promise of Home Rule for Ireland, but for some of the

Irish they had broken their promises too often to be credible. Moreover, if the rebels had succeeded, they would have taken Ireland out of the futile carnage of the First World War, thus saving lives rather than squandering them.

Political independence, however, came about only at the cost of more bloodshed, this time among the Irish themselves. Urged on by the Northern Protestants, the British government insisted on partitioning the island so that the more prosperous, mainly Protestant northern counties would stay within the United Kingdom. In fact the British Prime Minister of the day threatened the Irish with all-out war if they didn't knuckle under. The result was the formation of Northern Ireland, and a bloody civil war in the south between those who reluctantly accepted this arrangement – the followers of Michael Collins – and those who rejected it – the disciples of de Valera. The two major political parties in the country today, *Fine Gael* and *Fianna Fáil*, spring out of this conflict, and for a long time in Ireland what side your forefathers had fought on in the civil war was to matter a good deal.

Then, no sooner had the country won itself some peace and stability than the quarrel erupted again. In the late 1960s, war broke out in the North between those Catholics who had never accepted being cordoned off from those they saw as their fellow countrypeople in the south, and those Protestants who wanted to stay within the United Kingdom. The Treaty of 1921 which had won most of the country its independence also turned out to be a recipe for future disaster.

EASY-GOINGNESS

Not entirely a myth. The Irish can be as irascible and uptight as anyone else, but on the whole they're more relaxed about life than Berlin bankers and Surrey stockbrokers. This can be deeply annoying. If an Irish plumber says he'll fix your drains on Tuesday, it's quite likely he won't turn up. He may turn up on Friday, and won't think the delay worth mentioning. In fact he might get quite indignant if you bring it up. Friday is pretty close to Tuesday after all, even if your kitchen flooded and drowned your kids in the meanwhile.

Irish announcements like 'The meeting starts at eight o'clock sharp' are not to be taken literally, any more than statements like 'Jealousy is a green-eyed monster', or 'I was bowled over by his generosity'. Don't believe anyone who tells you (a) he'll ring, (b) he'll write, (c) the cheque is in the post. One of the most common lies in Ireland is 'we'll just go for one', meaning one drink in the pub. These are among the best known Irish fictions, James Joyce's *Ulysses* being one of the others.

On the other hand, all this has its advantages. If *you* happen to be three days late, chances are they won't even notice. Things in Ireland get done, but at a more leisurely pace than in Los Angeles. The Irish are not lazy, just laid-back. Some of them practise a philosophy known as Ahsurism, which isn't a brand of Buddhism but comes from the phrase 'Ah sure'. 'Ah sure, there's time enough ... Ah sure, it'll do later ...' And the personal touch will sometimes speed things up. If the decorators have been neglecting that damp bedroom for six months, tell them there's a new baby on the way and watch them move. This, however, is small comfort to some Vietnamese refugees in Ireland, who wrote to the government seventeen years ago requesting that their relatives be allowed to join them. They still haven't heard back.

Some of this laid-backness may be a residue of the old rural way of life. The point about having a small farm, as most of the Irish traditionally did, was that working harder wasn't especially profitable to you. There was no real relation between effort and reward. Planting more crops couldn't lower the rent you paid to the landlord. What mattered as far as wealth went was the size of the farm you had, not how much labour you put into it. And most Irish farms were tiny. So the Irish never saw the point of breaking their backs, and some of them still don't. At their best, the Irish work to live, unlike some other nations which live to work. At their worst, they're as mercenary as anyone else.

The Irish have as many rules as most other countries, but some of them are purely decorative. Centuries ago, an Irish

scholar boasted that there had been no law-breaking in his region for several decades. He didn't mention that there was no law either. A German friend of mine who went to register his car in Ireland was told to bring along documents to prove that he once lived in Germany but now lived in Dublin. This included two years of German phone, gas and electricity bills, the deed of sale for his home, letters from his solicitors, past and present employers and the like. Aghast at this prospect, he told the office that he was unable to oblige. 'Oh well', they shrugged, 'Just *some* of them then.' You can learn a lot about the Irish from that simple phrase.

EMIGRATION

The most popular pursuit in Ireland has always been how to get out of the place. Irish geography is unusual, in that the mountains are ringed around the coast rather than stacked in the middle. This is thought to be a way of trying to stop the natives from emigrating. Another way to keep them in was to pass an act of parliament forbidding them to leave the country, as happened in the Middle Ages. In traditional Ireland, only one son out of what was often a large bunch of children could inherit the family farm. The other children had either to become nuns and priests or go abroad, since there was precious little other work available in the country. Since the people who emigrated were often the most resourceful, enterprising ones, Ireland may have lost the flower of its population.[10] There were soon far more Irish people living outside the island than inside it. Today, over a

---

[10] FIF: Between the 1840s and the 1960s, an astonishing six million people left Ireland.

third of those born in Ireland are living overseas. Forty four million Americans claim to be of Irish descent, many of them of Scots-Irish background, and almost one third of all Australians. In fact between 1929 and 1949, five out of six Australian heads of government were of direct Irish ancestry.[11]

No less than two and a half million Irish men and women left the country between 1848 and 1855, in the wake of the Great Famine. Towards the close of the nineteenth century, only around 60% of people born in Ireland were still living there. Men and women left in more or less equal numbers, though many more women took the boat to Britain than they did to Australia and New Zealand. Only a small number of all the Irish who set sail had skills or capital resources; they were mostly classified as labourers or domestic servants. Their motives for leaving were probably mixed: in some cases dire necessity, but also perhaps the pull of a better life overseas. For some, it was a matter of enterprise rather than exile.[12] It's claimed, for example, that many Irish women who travelled to the United States came under this category. Not many of the Irish seemed to have emigrated for political reasons.

There were some well-established links between specific places in Ireland and particular overseas territories: Waterford and Newfoundland, Wexford and Argentina, Clare and Australia, Kerry and New Zealand, Derry and

---

[11] FIF: The founder of the Argentinian navy, William Brown, was a native of County Mayo, while Bernado O'Higgins, who hailed from County Offaly (see BIFFO), was a leader of the independence movement in Chile in the early nineteenth century.

[12] FIF: There was a higher death rate for Irish immigrants into British and US cities than there had been in Famine-ridden rural Ireland.

Philadelphia. In the 1930s, one village in county Clare was kept economically afloat by the Shanghai police force. One of its inhabitants had sailed off to become an officer there, and other villagers flocked out to join him. Fares to Canada were lower than those to the USA, and Britain was the option of some of the poorer emigrants because it was far cheaper to get to. But some of them might also have chosen it because they forlornly imagined it would be easier to return home. Quite a few others, however, came to Britain as a stepping stone to settling elsewhere.

Though few immigrants actually did return home, they seem to have been quite socially mobile in the places they washed up in. There were settled Irish neighbourhoods abroad, but lots of people drifted in and out of them. On the whole, Irish immigrants seem to have adjusted impressively well to their new conditions. They were often adept at securing what was known as the best of the worst jobs. The United States received more Irish immigrants than anywhere else, which usually meant that the newcomers had to transform themselves from a rural to an urban people.[13] In fact by 1890, only 2% of Irish immigrants in the States were involved in agriculture, and the picture was similar in Britain. By 1855, the Irish made up over a third of the population of New York. Yet they didn't cling to the east coast, spreading out instead to the mid-west, the south, the mountain states and the west coast.

It's something of a myth that the Irish abroad lived in ghettoes. Exclusively Irish streets, much less whole Irish neighbourhoods, were actually quite rare. Most of those who

---

[13] FIF: In 1870, the Irish were the largest first-generation immigrant group in 27 of the most populous US cities.

sailed to Canada were Protestants, as were a high proportion of those who travelled to Scotland and New Zealand. Indeed some historians think that the image of the Irish-American Catholic is in much need of revision. Because of the cross-border flow from Canada, so they claim, the bulk of the Irish-American population has always been Protestant in background, though this has got squeezed out of the official histories.

Even so, Catholicism remained mightily important. It was the chief way in which Irish immigrants could cling on to their national identity, given that only a small minority of them engaged in nationalist politics. The Irish abroad kept up an attachment to their faith as a way of sustaining their culture. It was also a defence against what many of them saw rather sniffily as a godless, materialist environment. A lot of immigrants tended to marry within the ethnic group. In some places, there was even a preference for marriage partners from the same part of Ireland. In all these ways, immigrants could try to come to terms with the uprootedness, loneliness, insecurity, blocked social mobility and sense of alienation that so many of them experienced. They were also of course sometimes the targets of vicious racist prejudice, which in turn helped to foster social and political solidarity.

The Irish imported their political machine into the United States – indeed it was one of their major gifts to American culture – but some studies suggest that their social progress there was slow and erratic. There's also some evidence that the Irish abroad were less concerned with 'getting on' than some other ethnic groups.

A different pattern of emigration continues today. Many of those who leave tend to be aspiring middle-class townsfolk rather than downtrodden rural labourers, and a lot of them emigrate only for a few years. It's more of a brain drain than a matter of survival. But aside from these NIPPLEs (New Irish Professional People Living in England), non-voluntary emigration is still disturbingly high, and perhaps a quarter of a million young Irish people are thought to be living illegally in the USA. All this provides a vital safety-valve for the Irish economy, making it look more buoyant than it probably is. Around 20,000 young people are estimated to have emigrated between 1982 and 1992. There are still large working-class Irish ghettoes in Britain. In fact three-quarters of Britain's building trade is owned by people with an Irish background. 'Paddy' in Britain is still thought of as a bricklayer rather than an architect.[14] A lot of the Irish in Britain are nostalgic for home, and have to put up with racial insults. In the days immediately following an IRA bombing in Britain, it was sometimes safer for the Irish not to open their mouths in public and betray their nationality.

Emigration has etched a deep wound in the Irish psyche. For one thing, it has intensified the solitude and sense of failure of those left at home. It's deeply demoralising to be part of a country which everyone around you seems to be abandoning like a leaky raft. At the same time, it's been responsible for a great deal of psychological damage for those who found themselves without a penny in alien, often hostile places. The Irish are a proud, sometimes prickly people, and don't take easily to being defined as spongers and 'blow-ins'(new arrivals). Some of them were taught to look down on the godless Anglo-Saxons as their spiritual inferiors, and having to do their dirty work for them was thus

---

[14] FIF: Of all ethnic groups in England, the Irish die youngest, have the second highest suicide rate, and the highest rate of entry to psychiatric hospitals.

particularly rankling. Some emigrants, especially to the States, developed a morbid nostalgia for home, fully of fantasy, false heroics and sickly sentimentalism. Yet this starry-eyedness didn't prevent them from scrambling into positions of power in their adopted countries, which they would never have dreamed of abandoning to return home. Like many Irish phenomena, emigration has its element of double-think. You may want to check out your Irish forefathers in the National Library, but would you really want to live here? You may have enjoyed the ring of Kerry, but have they told you about that steep rate of income tax?

One of the more frustrating aspects of Irish emigration is well known to regular users of the National Library in Dublin. As the tourist season gets under way, the desk becomes jammed with people of Irish descent seeking out their ancestors. Sometimes all they have to go on is a little piece of paper on which are written the words 'Murphy, Mayo', which they solemnly hand to the long-suffering librarians. This is one good reason to wish that the emigrants had all bloody well stayed at home.

FAIRIES

It is a myth that there are fairies in Ireland. There used to be, but not any more. According to folklore, the last great convention of the Irish fairies took place in 1839. They decided that their existence was no longer necessary in a rapidly modernising country, and sailed out of Ireland the following day. Nobody is sure where they went, but some suggest San Francisco.

FAMINE

The word 'Famine' in Ireland usually refers to the Great Famine of 1845-49, which killed about a million people and drove millions more into exile over the following two decades. Those who perished, as usual with famines, died more of disease than starvation. But there have been quite a few famines in Irish history, some of them perhaps even more severe than what has become known as the Great Hunger. What makes that event unique is that firstly it lasted longer than most other Irish famines – the potato crop failed year after year – and secondly that it covered so much of the country. Some regions, however, were much more afflicted than others; conditions in west Cork, Mayo and Donegal were especially catastrophic, much more so than in the east of the country. The small town of Clonakilty in west Cork was particularly badly hit, and for some years afterwards older people in Ireland, when mentioning the name of the town, would add the phrase 'God help us'. You may come across the odd Famine graveyard in your travels, pits where people were buried together without coffins. Coffins cost money, so a special type was used with a sliding bottom, which could tip the corpse out and then be used again.

Today in Ireland, the Famine is, like many other things, a source of contention. What you think about it can reveal whether you are a nationalist or a critic of nationalism, and so has a direct bearing on the politics of today. For some Irish, those who still mourn the Famine are morbidly fixated on the past, and in accusing England of genocide succeed only in buttressing the cause of the IRA. According to them, Ireland at the time was desperately overpopulated, and the Famine was a natural, perhaps unavoidable disaster simply waiting to happen. The Irish people were far too dependent on a single crop, the potato; they cultivated other crops, but these they had to sell in order to pay the landlord his rent. The British government, so it's claimed, did its best to tackle the tragedy, but given the enormous scale of the suffering, no government of the day could have adequately resolved it.

Famines are not generally caused by food shortages. In most famines, there is enough food around the place; the problem lies in bringing the food and the hungry people together. Famines are usually caused by people's inability to buy food, not by its total absence. Whether this was so of the Great Famine depends on your point of view. The bug which blighted the potato crop year after year seems to have caused an absolute food shortage in the country. Some nationalists point angrily to the fact that food nevertheless went on being exported to Britain during the Famine; there are poignant accounts of desperate men and women attacking food convoys and being beaten off by British soldiers. But some historians claim that keeping this food in the country might not have made that much difference, and that more food was imported than exported during the Famine years.

But there is another case to consider. There may not have been enough food available in Ireland itself; but there was more than enough in the United Kingdom as a whole. And Ireland at the time was supposed to be part of that kingdom. The British government, however, insisted on treating the Famine as a specifically Irish problem, and threw much of the responsibility for dealing with it on the Irish landlords, many of whom were in dire financial straits themselves. Would they have done something similar if a famine had broken out in Kent or Yorkshire? Yet Ireland, officially at least, was just as much part of Britain as those counties.

In any case, it's hard to argue that the British relief operation was anything like adequate, even by the standards of the time. Even some high-placed British officials didn't think so. The government set up food depots, then closed them again. They provided soup kitchens, but only after thousands of lives had been lost. Trusting dogmatically to the workings of the free market, they refused for a long time to distribute free food for fear it would undermine private enterprise. They spent a mere £10 million on famine relief, compared with the £70 million they spent on their war in the Crimea. Most criminally of all, they declared the Famine officially over long before it was. And if so many of the Irish people were dependent solely on the potato, wasn't this something to do with the social system which Britain and the Irish landlords ran in the country?

It's hard to credit that the British deliberately planned genocide, as some Irish nationalists claim. But some historians believe that they could have saved Ireland, at least from the worst of the disaster, if they had had the will to do so. The reason why they hadn't is probably because feeding the hungry was not in fact their main priority. Instead, they glimpsed in the Famine a golden opportunity for a long-term restructuring of the ailing Irish economy – one that would clear away inefficient landlords and tenants, get rid of unviably small farms through death and eviction, and allow these holdings to be consolidated into larger, more viable units which would lessen the country's dependence on the uncivilised potato. This, in fact, is what eventually happened, and the Irish landlords played their brutal part by evicting thousands of small farmers during those years.

Difficult though it is to believe, some in the British government detected in this terrible catastrophe the hand of divine Providence. Unfortunately for the Irish, this included the official in charge of the relief operation. They saw it as a blessing in disguise – God's own way of dragging the benighted Irish into the modern age. One of England's most distinguished economists (Nassau Senior) was heard to observe that he feared that a million dead in Ireland would 'scarcely be enough to do much good'. Whether you call this genocide or not perhaps depends on how you define the word.

The Famine was the death of many things besides a million people. It almost spelled the death of the Irish language, since most of those who died or emigrated were the poor, which meant on the whole the Irish speakers. After the Famine, there were those in the country who could speak Irish but didn't, regarding it as bad luck. The Irish language had already been on the wane before the Famine, partly because of the spreading influence of English, partly because it was a badge of shame associated with poverty and ignorance. (One Irishman of the time who was asked whether he spoke Irish replied stiffly that he might be ignorant, but not *that* ignorant.) But the Famine certainly gave the language a hefty kick towards the grave, until an outfit known as the Gaelic League struggled bravely to revive it at the end of the nineteenth century. The tragedy also put paid to a good deal of traditional culture, though this had been dying on its feet for some time too. Ireland after the Famine was probably a more sober, prudent, less festive place, obsessed with land ownership, deferring marriage until middle age, sternly regulating its sexual reproduction for fear once more of overpopulating the land.

Another thing the Famine put paid to was any lingering respect there might have been for the British or the landlords, who were now reviled and discredited. It was also the beginnings of the Irish nation abroad, especially in the United States, and it stirred up a smouldering hatred of the British which was to take the form of the revolutionary Irish

Republican Brotherhood. When the IRB struck for political freedom in 1916, a process which had started with the Famine came to its fruition. The event traumatised the Irish people, and there are those who believe that their collective psyche, if they have such a thing, has never fully recovered from it. But if the Famine meant forced emigration and the dreaded 'coffin' ships on which so many refugees died, it was also the birth of a new, more self-confident Irish nation overseas. It helped to internationalise the Irish, turning them outwards to a world beyond their own narrow island.

Today, there is a National Famine Museum at Strokestown, County Roscommon, which contains at least two dark ironies. One is that the museum is set in a Big House whose landlord evicted about 3,000 people during the Great Hunger, and was assassinated by his tenants as a consequence. The other irony is that the visitor finally emerges into rather a good restaurant.

FEET, LEFT AND RIGHT

In Northern Ireland, the question 'Which foot do you dig with?' means 'Are you a Catholic or a Protestant?' Catholics are said to dig with the left foot, Protestants with the right. The origin of this quaint expression can be traced to the fact that two different kinds of spade were traditionally used in Ireland, one in (mainly Catholic) Munster and Connacht, and the other in (partly Protestant) Ulster. One of the spades had a notch on the left for the digging foot, while the other had the notch on the right. Unfortunately, the popular expression gets things the wrong way round. It was the 'Catholic' spade which had a notch on the right, and the 'Protestant' one which had it on the left.

Some Northerners believe that there are a score of different ways of telling Protestants and Catholics apart, aside from obvious ones like where you live, which school you attended and what you're called. Someone called Siobhan Murphy is unlikely to be a Protestant, while not many Catholics are called Willy Hanna. But there are more subtle forms of distinction too: for example, Catholics in the North, like people in the Republic, tend to pronounce the letter *aitch* as *haitch*.

The tale is told of a tourist in Belfast who fell into the hands of a drunken sectarian mob. 'Are you a Protestant or a Catholic?' they demanded, thrusting him against a wall. 'Neither,' he stammered, 'I'm an atheist.' 'But are you a Protestant atheist or a Catholic atheist?' they insisted.

Don't, by the way, let this story scare you off from visiting the North. They've been far too busy fighting each other to bother with the likes of you.

FUGGHAN

The Irish way of pronouncing a well-known swear-word. The Irish swear a good deal more than a lot of other nations, though this is partly a class matter. Some working-class and lower-middle-class Irish say 'fugghan' as often as the English say 'sorry', the French say 'Alors' and the Americans say 'Hi'. This is because it has ceased to be a swear-word for them and has become a meaningless filling-in word instead, similar to 'Like' for some young Americans. This may be taken either as evidence of Irish virtue, or of the fact that the country has an ancient tradition of ferocious cursing. Irish bards could shrivel your eyeballs and slay your cattle with one well-placed imprecation. The frequency of 'fugghan' has no connection with the fact that, judging from the number of children around, there is a fair amount of copulation in Ireland. Given the astonishingly high levels of Irish fertility, there may be no more acts of copulation in the place than there are children, which is admittedly a lot, but could be a lot more.

GAELIC

Visitors to Ireland are often keen to hear Gaelic spoken.[15] The more correct term is in fact 'Irish', since there are different kinds of Gaelic spoken elsewhere. Irish people who refer to the language as Gaelic are sometimes signalling a hostility to the culture it symbolises. Almost all the Irish learn their native language at school, but outside the Irish-speaking areas, a lot of them speak it about as well as they and the Anglo-Saxons speak French, i.e. atrociously. The Irish language has been dying for a long time, for a number of reasons:

1. The Great Famine, as we've seen, killed off mostly the poorer Irish, and these were mostly the Irish speakers. It also drove millions of other poor Irish speakers into exile. Though in fact the language was already in decline before the Famine set in.

2. Irish, unlike Guinness, was not good for you. If you wanted to get on in business or the professions, or emigrate to Britain, Australia or the States, speaking English gave you a head start. Though this isn't enough reason in itself for the decline of the native tongue.

---

[15] FIF: The word 'Gaelic' probably derives from a Welsh word meaning 'wild, untamed'.

Many small nations, like Denmark and Finland, have learnt a more widely-spoken language without abandoning their own.

3. British colonial rule in Ireland was often hostile to the native culture, including the Irish language, and either suppressed or discouraged it. But some of the Irish co-operated willingly enough with this project. Moreover, just as the Irish language was being revived at the end of the last century, some of the greatest literature in English which the country had ever witnessed sprang up with excessively bad timing.

4. When most of Ireland finally became an independent nation earlier this century, Irish governments forced through a ham-fisted, unrealistic policy for reviving the language. Many children who were forced to learn it at school found it a tedious chore and forgot it as soon as they could, along with equilateral triangles and de Valera's birth date. According to the constitution, Irish is still the first official language of the country, but this is another Irish fiction, like saying that you've had your dinner when you haven't. (It's also believed in some quarters that the Irish constitution itself, a document supposedly written in Irish, was in fact first written in English and then translated.) Around 30% of the Irish report on census returns that they can speak the language, but whether they would be able to say so in Irish is debatable.

5. Ireland is too close to Britain not to be influenced by the English language, and nowadays is too culturally close to the States. But the Welsh have fared better at preserving their language than the Irish, and there's not even a stretch of sea between them and the English. Because they speak English, the Irish are vulnerable to a

lot of trashy English-language films, music, TV programmes and newspapers; but the fact that they speak English has also helped to catapult them to the centre of the international cultural stage, particularly in writing, the cinema and popular music. So there are gains to outweigh the losses.

6. Learning the Irish language is sometimes associated these days with militant nationalism. This is one reason why some of the Irish have been wary of taking it up. And since most of the country is now independent, there's less reason for emphasising it anyway. National languages are often ways of asserting one's identity against a greater political power, as with the use of Catalan in north-east Spain. But since the Republic of Ireland has now been free of British authority for almost eighty years, there's less incentive to use the language as a badge of political belonging.

7. To learn Irish requires major brain surgery. It is a wonderfully rich, subtle, expressive tongue, but not at all easy to pick up. Example: the word *Tanaiste*, meaning deputy prime minister, is pronounced something like 'Tawnishta'. The word for the prime minister, *Taoiseach*, is pronounced 'Tee-shuck'. This is not to be confused with 'tea-shop', which is an English rather than Irish institution. Even so, most foreigners who have lived in the country for some years usually pick up a word or two of the language. Aer Lingus, for example.

Most Irish people who speak Irish as their first language live in areas known as the Gaeltachts, which are mostly along the western seaboard. Today, about 30,000 people in these regions, a mere 1% of the total population, speak Irish as their first language. Monoglot speakers – i.e. those who speak nothing but Irish – died out in the last century. The Gaeltachts are declining, but there's been a modest resurgence of Irish speaking in the country as a whole. There are more and more schools which do all their teaching in Irish, writers who write only in Irish, and lots of individual enthusiasts who might brush up their Irish in evening classes. The language is growing fastest among the nationalist communities of Northern Ireland, who learn it to affirm their cultural identity.

You may find a lot of Dubliners who seem to be speaking Irish, but this is just because their English can be hard for the tourist to understand. If someone says to you 'ya fugghan gobshoite', this, believe it or not, is actually English. Don't hang around too long if you hear this phrase.

GAY BYRNE

Ireland's leading broadcaster recently retired, chat show host and former of public opinion. Possibly the most important man in the country. See GOD.

GIANT'S CAUSEWAY

The third big disappointment of the trip. The great English writer Samuel Johnson was once asked whether it was worth seeing. 'Worth seeing, sir,' he replied, 'Not worth going to see.' He was probably right. Don't break your neck to view this mildly interesting stack of rocks. But since the area surrounding it, the coasts and glens of Antrim, is well worth going to see, it would be churlish not to cast a glance at the

Causeway too. The rock formation includes what looks like an organ, said to have been played twice a year by legendary giant Finn MacCool, once on July 12 (a day sacred to Northern Irish Protestants) and once on March 17 (the Catholic feast day of St. Patrick). This makes Finn the first of a long line of liberals who thought they could please both sides in the Northern conflict. He failed because back then the conflict hadn't actually started; others have failed because it started too long ago.

SOMEHOW IT NEVER CAUGHT ON.

THE DWARF'S CAUSEWAY.

GOD

An astonishingly popular figure in Ireland, second only to Bono, lead singer of the rock group U2. A few years ago, 98% of Irish Catholics said that they believed in God. This was Catholics, not the Irish in general, so one wonders what the other 2% of Catholics believed in. And the Irish are twice as likely to believe in heaven, hell and the devil as any other European people. Since the decline of the Irish language, Catholicism has become the single most important mark of Irish identity, which is one reason why it's so tenacious. Although the society is rapidly becoming more secular, not least among its hordes of youth, the Irish still rank among the most pious people in the world, to judge from their remarkably high rate of Mass attendance. Some years ago it was running at well above 80%, as opposed to a mere 13% for supposedly Catholic France. Today, however, it has sunk on some estimates to 55%. And the fact that the alternative to going to church might be going to hell is a great incentive for getting out of bed on a Sunday morning. Attendance at confession is still high, despite its sometimes embarrassing aspects. ('Where did he touch you, my child?' 'On the canal bank, Father.')

Some 95% of the Irish are baptised Catholics. If you're sitting on top of a bus and everyone suddenly crosses themselves, it's because you're passing a church. Years ago, the stewardesses on Aer Lingus, the Irish airline, had to be ordered to stop crossing themselves when the plane took off. It wasn't the most reassuring sight for the passengers. Some of the Irish have even been known to cross themselves when passing a post office, post offices having become sacred places since the main one in Dublin formed the scene in 1916 for the insurrection which led to political independence (see

EASTER RISING) But a lot of the Irish these days are more likely to cross themselves while passing a bank.

Ireland is strewn with convents, shrines, monasteries, dancing or weeping statues of the Virgin, just as the streets are thronged with men and women in fancy dress known as priests and nuns.[16] Priests were traditionally given a wide berth because they were thought to have the power to turn you into a donkey, blight your crops, or wither your limbs if you disobeyed their dictates. These days they are more likely to be given a wide berth because they're suspected of being child abusers. There are probably more saints in the country than psychiatrists, some of them dealing in specialist requests such as the curing of throat disease or how to find a lost handbag. On the whole, however, it's better when praying not to deal with sub-committees but to go straight to the Management.

Catholicism believes in absolute values, but the Irish are fairly relative about them. Opinion polls suggest that they're more likely to hold to strict distinctions between good and bad than other European nations, though most ordinary Irish people aren't censorious. They are a deeply religious people, but they are not on the whole ranters, fanatics and moralisers like US evangelists, or smug and oily like some Anglican clergy in England. The early Celtic church was fairly laid-back about authority, sexuality and the role of women; St Brigid might even have been a bishop. It tended to see God

---

[16] FIF: Ireland's main shrine to the Virgin is Knock in Mayo, said to be the third biggest in Europe after Lourdes and Fatima. It even has its own international airport. When the Virgin Mary put in an appearance there in 1879, the story goes that the parish priest didn't even bother going to look at her, assured that she was always around his church in any case.

more as a liberator than a judge. Today, religion in Ireland is no obstacle to having a good time. The Irish manage to combine a belief in absolutes with a tolerance for human frailty, which is one of their specialities. The Irish warm to failure more than they do to success, which they tend to begrudge. In general, they are serious but not sanctimonious about their faith.

Believing in God doesn't necessarily mean believing in the bishop, or even in the pope. In fact it was a pope who granted an English king his title to Ireland in the Middle Ages, and who wrote to congratulate him on his military victory. 'You have wonderfully and gloriously triumphed over the people of Ireland,' he wrote, 'who destroy themselves in mutual slaughter ... a race uncivilised and undisciplined.' But the Irish are a forgiving bunch: when Pope John Paul XIII visited the place, most of the population turned out to cheer him. Apart from Vatican city, Ireland must be one of the few states in the world where a majority of the inhabitants have actually clapped eyes on the Roman pontiff.

Like many Catholic nations, however, the country has a long, robust anti-clerical tradition, despite having almost as many clergy per square yard as Vatican city. It also has its fair share of radical priests and nuns, who are deeply critical of the official church. One survey shows that more Irish Catholics believe in the need for radical change in the church than the citizens of any other Catholic country. This is probably less evidence of Irish radicalism than of the shocking state of their church. It's often thought that the Catholic Church in Ireland has a stranglehold over state policy, telling the government what to do. This is a myth: statistics show that the Irish bishops have interfered in very few political decisions. Constitutionally speaking, the

Catholic Church no longer has a privileged place in Irish society. But its unofficial power is still fairly formidable. Quite recently, an Irish bishop declared in a surge of Christian humility that 'We, the bishops, are Christ'. Today, however, more and more of the Irish would like to know whether Christ sees himself as the Irish bishops.

Mass attendance, as we have seen, is declining, especially among the youth, the unemployed, those in urban areas, and the better-educated. In fact without unemployment, which makes you reluctant to join in social rituals, mass attendance would probably be significantly higher. So the causes of 'secularisation' in Ireland don't just lie in the spread of 'enlightened' views; in some ways the reverse is true. The authority of the Catholic Church has been plunged into crisis by a series of spectacular sexual scandals. Gone are the days when a priest remarked that he knew many happily married couples who had abstained from sexual intercourse for twenty years. And the gloomy truth is that Ireland hasn't had an officially approved miracle since the Virgin Mary put in a frustratingly brief appearance in the small town of Knock in 1879. This is an embarrassingly long time for one of the most pious nations on earth to be without an authorised miracle. God ought to see to it immediately.

It's hard to leave the Catholic Church entirely, however, since the church has a category to cover such people, known as 'lapsed'. This is a way of making sure that those outside it are still somehow inside. The church is thus a body you can never really resign from, since resignation just shifts you from one category to another, like being a country rather than a city member of a club. Being a lapsed Catholic puts you in some highly distinguished company and in some people's view comes only a little below the saints. In descending order of importance, there is God, then the saints, then lapsed Catholics, then the clergy, then the simple faithful, then Protestants. But even Protestants would be Catholics if only they'd stop reading the bible.

Judging from the brisk trade in chemist shops, most of the Irish seem not to be ruffled by the fact that contraception is officially a mortal sin. Divorce is a mortal sin too, but the Irish state now allows it, and people co-habit quite openly, as they did in medieval times. Abortion is illegal, but most of the Irish are in favour of distributing information about how to get an abortion in Britain. It's a question of bending the rules again, even when the rules are thought up by God.

GONNE, MAUD

One of the many Irish phenomena which are real and mythical at the same time. Maud Gonne was born in England, the daughter of a British army officer. At the age of fourteen she accepted a proposal of marriage made to her by moonlight in the Coliseum in Rome, though her parents had other plans for her immediate future. Later, through her French lover, she fell in with an unsavoury bunch of French right-wing anti-Semites, and embarked on a cloak-and-dagger mission to Russia to enlist the Tsar's support for a political conspiracy against the French government. Despite her later radicalism, Gonne was to retain some unpleasant right-wing anti-Semitic leanings, and to view all things British as the work of the devil.

Shifting her scene to Ireland, she became deeply embroiled in the campaign against evictions in the west. She encountered the poet William Yeats, and in his own words 'struck him like a gong'. Yeats fell hopelessly in love with her, though whether the relationship was ever consummated is a matter for scholarly debate. The couple would sometimes lie together with their ears to the ground, listening to the music of the fairies. At least that's what they *said* they were doing. Much to Yeats's chagrin, however, Maud married the alcoholic lout John MacBride, whose only achievement in life was to get himself shot by the British for his part in the Easter Rising. While honeymooning with MacBride, Gonne concocted a plot to assassinate Queen Victoria, having not much else to do.

When the plot came to nothing, Gonne was forced to content herself with campaigning against Queen Victoria's state visit to Ireland, and had her first taste of police brutality. She embarked on a fiery lecture tour of the USA, before returning to the west to help organise famine relief. She was elected president of the Irish women's republican movement, and became a close friend of the working-class socialist James Connolly, who was also to be executed for his part in the Easter Rising. (Connolly had a pronounced squint, which came from trying to read as a child in a poor home without adequate light.) Gonne acted in nationalist plays, and campaigned for the children of the poor. She was jailed in 1917, but turned the tables on the British judicial system by later becoming a judge in the (then illegal) Sinn Fein courts.

During the civil war following independence, Gonne nursed casualties and launched a women's defence league for Republican prisoners known as The Mothers. In 1932, her work on behalf of prisoners was rewarded when the Irish government emptied the jails of political convicts. Maud helped found the Workers Party of Ireland, hooked up with Indian nationalists, and supported women's rights against the patriarchal Irish Free State. She died in 1953, late enough to see Ireland sever its final political links with the United

Kingdom. Throughout her turbulent career, she preserved two favourite ball gowns from her days as a debutante.

GUBU

Journalese for 'Grotesque, Unbelievable, Bizarre and Unprecedented'. These were the words with which a former Irish Prime Minister greeted the news that a criminal on the run from the police had been found in the home of his attorney general. This is a bit like discovering that your Minister for Education can't read, or that your Minister of Health has contracted AIDS. The Irish are well accustomed to political scandals, but this seemed to be pushing things a bit far.

HAPPINESS

Despite wet weather, the price of Guinness, the fact that there was a war going on just to the north of them for almost thirty years, and the fact that much of the world sees them as liars and layabouts, the Irish are a happy people. How do we know? We know from the results of a 1990 opinion poll which tested people's sense of satisfaction with life. Over nine out of ten Irish respondents to the poll indicated that they were happy. This contrasts with downright miserable nations like Spain, Italy, France and Portugal, whose climate obviously isn't enough to lift their spirits. It also raises the ticklish philosophical question of whether you are happy if you think you are. The Irish have a tendency to put a good face on things, smirking cheerily while being savaged by a mongoose; but even so, these results are striking. Older people in Ireland were on the whole happier than younger ones, and women who were house-workers were generally happier than those who weren't. The Irish scored splendidly in terms of how much they trusted other people, and a high percentage of them took pride in being Irish. Being a Paddy is clearly better than Prozac.

HEANEY, SEAMUS

One of the best-known living Irishmen, and one of the country's major exports. Heaney has a workshop in Dublin where he manufactures delectable morsels known as poems, which are shipped all over the world and should reach you in pristine condition. Some of them slip down easily, while others require some chewing and digesting. All the items are hand-made and have an authentic Irish flavour. Likely to be remembered for a lot longer than Bob Geldof.

HEDGE SCHOOLS

During the Penal Era in the eighteenth century, Catholics were forbidden by the British authorities to run schools. Instead, they educated some of their children in places known as hedge schools, so-called because in good weather they met out in the open. Poor peasant children were famed for their knowledge of Virgil and Homer, though a lot of this may be mythical. There are many stories of Irish children walking three or four miles barefoot to school in the countryside, which probably aren't mythical. The Irish are well-known for their respect for learning, and many a poor family would give a bed for the night to a wandering scholar.[17] Edmund Burke, the greatest political thinker Ireland ever produced, and one of the finest orators the House of Commons has ever witnessed, started life in a hedge school in County Cork.

On the other hand, hedge schools weren't always as romantic as they sound. Like most Irish romances, this one too has its unsavoury underside. Some of the schoolmasters were drunks, frauds and pedants, bamboozling their pupils with high-sounding nonsense. Children could be brutally beaten. Later on, national schools were established by the state for all Irish children, but they were rightly suspected by the people as instruments of British propaganda. The study of Irish history and literature were banned, and a hymn sung by the students told of the joy of being 'a happy English child'.

In some of these schools, the children were required to wear a wooden stick around their necks. A child who used a word of Irish would have a notch cut in his or her stick by the teacher, and at the end of the day the child with the greatest number of notches would be beaten. This was a somewhat unsubtle way of knocking the Irish language out of them. But the teachers who did this were usually Irish themselves, and many of the children's Irish-speaking parents would probably have approved. Like any parents, they wanted their children to get on in life, and that meant learning English.

There are no hedge schools in Ireland today, but there are four universities. These are Trinity College, the National University (which has campuses in Dublin, Galway,

---

[17] FIF: 10,000 Dublin workers are said to have marched to lay the foundation stone of the Catholic University in 1862.

Maynooth and Cork), and two technically-oriented universities in Dublin and Limerick. Trinity College is by far the oldest of them, founded in the late sixteenth century by Queen Elizabeth I. The main building you see, though, is mid-eighteenth century. For most of its career, the college was a fortress of English Protestant power in Ireland. Catholics weren't allowed in for a long time, and then, when they were, the Catholic bishops banned them from attending. This is an intriguing variant on the old Groucho Marx joke that he wouldn't join a club which let in people like himself. Trinity was a kind of Oxford-by-the-Liffey, full of English and Anglo-Irish aristocrats who were too dim to get into the real place. A lot of them spent their time playing cricket and croquet and leaping off roofs with a gallon of beer inside them. At one time, the place was known as the 'silent sister' of Oxford and Cambridge, meaning that you never heard a peep out of it. The professors were too busy swilling sherry and tucking into roast boar to bother with anything as vulgar as reading books, let alone writing them.

Even so, Trinity produced a glittering array of Ireland's leading writers and thinkers, from Jonathan Swift and Edmund Burke to Oscar Wilde and Samuel Beckett. Nowadays 90% of the students are Catholic, and it's an eminent place of learning, though horrendously overcrowded. Trapped in the centre of town, it can't easily expand. The place has about 10,000 students, which would be like packing the whole of Oxford University into a single Oxford college. Its excellent library is as crammed with bodies as a football stadium. The only book most tourists will see is the Book of Kells, which along with the bible is one of the most revered and least read books in the world.

Levels of education in Ireland are generally quite high, though in some areas – maths, science, modern languages –

the country has lagged behind. There are almost one million school students out of a total population of three and a half million, a higher proportion than in any comparable country. This enormous number of minds to educate has strained the resources of a traditionally poor country to its limits. School buildings are often ill-equipped and resources scanty, though teachers receive a fairly decent salary and are granted reasonably high status. Average *per capita* spending on education comes well down on the international list, and staff/student ratios are worse than in most other European countries. Education in Ireland isn't cheap, and parents often have to finance their children, which means that the children of the less well-off have been scandalously under-represented in higher education (although recently this has somewhat improved). Children start school at the early age of four, and schools are still mostly run by religious denominations, though funded largely by the state. Some 80% of secondary schools are owned and controlled by Catholic religious orders, and there is a handful of posh boarding schools.

HIMSELF/HERSELF

Like a lot of words in a language, the Irish meaning of these terms can really only be picked up by hearing them used. 'Himself' can mean the man of the family, as in 'Himself will be wanting his breakfast'. But it can also refer to any important male figure around the place, or just to a particular male under discussion. The same goes for 'Herself', which can mean the wife or mother of the family, or, more generally, some significant female. Only the context makes it clear which of these is intended. A man's surname prefixed by 'The', as in 'The O'Donoghue', indicates that he is the senior male member of his clan.

There are other Irish usages which can only be grasped in context, such as adding 'so' to the end of a sentence: 'I'll put the suitcase there, so'. There's also a soft intake of breath, which hovers somewhere between a sign of agreement and a poignant expression of feeling. This is more common with women than men, and much less common among the young.

HISTORY

Like pubs and litter, there's too much of this around in Ireland. History for the British means how they have always done things; for some of the Irish it means how they have

always been done. They have an appallingly tragic history of war, foreign occupation, insurrection, famine, religious persecution, grinding poverty, and buses which never run on time. You can see, then, why they're also the wittiest people in the world. Without their wit they would all just leap *en masse* into Dublin bay.

It's a myth, however, that the Irish are all obsessed with their history. Even in the North, history is mainly a way of clashing over current issues. It's true that many of the Irish have a keener sense of their history than other nations, partly because there's so much of it around, and partly because it's still an important factor in moulding the present. In 1998, the two hundredth anniversary of the United Irish uprising, a team of Irish historians travelled the country speaking about the event to a mixed bag of audiences, including the Wexford hurling team. But quite a lot of the Irish are no more interested in their own history than Bill Gates is interested in the Pilgrim Fathers. History today in Ireland is rapidly becoming a commodity packaged for the consumption of tourists. As often, what looks like something for the Irish turns out to be something for the visitor.

There is, however, one way in which the Irish view of history is different from the English. For the English, an injustice which took place in the past will gradually fade from memory with the passage of time. For some Irish ways of thinking, past injustices linger on in the present. They don't go away just because they happened a long time ago. Some Irish farmers in the nineteenth century who had had their land confiscated by the British two centuries or so before, still believed it to be rightfully theirs. The Irish are a conservative race, not the anarchists or revolutionists they're sometimes portrayed as. Even their use of violence was often an attempt to get back to some previous state of affairs, or to preserve the status quo. On the other hand, opinion polls suggest that with the exception of their negative views on abortion and sexual permissiveness, the Irish aren't particularly more conservative than other Europeans.

HORSES

If the English are crazy about dogs, the Irish are demented about horses. Horses in Ireland are a religion as much as a sport, a spiritual cult as well as an immensely lucrative industry. The country is commonly thought to be the best place in the world to breed them, and horse-breeders in Ireland now include a clutch of Arab multi-millionaires.

Some of the old-style Anglo-Irish gentry seemed to get off
their horses only to go to bed, and even then showed definite
signs of wanting to drag them between the sheets. Some of
them certainly seemed to prefer four legs to two, even if the
two legs in question held up their wives and children. In the
Anglo-Irish Jonathan Swift's novel *Gulliver's Travels*, horses
are a race of supremely rational beings, far superior to
humans. The Irish playwright Brendan Behan once described
an Anglo-Irish gentleman as a Protestant on a horse.

There are stud farms galore on the rich central pastures of
the country, and 27 racecourses attended by over one million
punters a year. Irish horses are one of the nation's most
glamorous, desirable exports, along with Sinead O'Connor
and Pierce Brosnan. They bring in about £65 million
annually in sales. The Dublin Horse Show is one of the
glittering social events of the year, while in the countryside
traditional hunts flourish. Horse racing in Ireland prides itself
on being a more classless pursuit than it is in England,
though this is questionable: the industry has traditionally
been controlled by a tight group of military-style gentlemen.

INVENTORS

It's a little known fact that an Irishman invented the world's
first dirigible torpedo. Irishmen also invented the steam
turbine engine, the nuclear particle generator, the landing
craft used on D-Day in the Second World War, shorthand,
the submarine, and the first practical use of colour
photography. The world's first tank was co-designed by a
Dubliner, and it was an Irishman who first explained why
the sky is blue. This last fact is particularly puzzling, since
the sky in Ireland is rarely blue. The word 'bureaucracy' was
coined by an Irish writer, Lady Morgan.

Most of these facts are quite unknown, largely because they are boring. But some of the more nationalistic Irish are pressing to have them more widely broadcast around the world, perhaps by printing stamps portraying nuclear particle generators, blue skies and snatches of shorthand. There's also a campaign to erect a statue of a dirigible torpedo in Dublin's O'Connell Street, once it's been ascertained exactly what it is. Some Irish nationalists believe that an Irishman reached the moon long before the Americans, and planted a statue of the Blessed Virgin there, which powerful telescopes can just make out. Another famous Irish inventor was St Brendan (see BRENDAN THE NAVIGATOR), who according to some legends discovered a hitherto unknown phenomenon called America. A great deal of invention has also been known to take place from time to time in Irish pub conversation.

Another Irish invention was the mass political movement. Mass politics, at least in Europe, was the brainchild of the nineteenth-century nationalist lawyer Daniel O'Connell, whose statue, bullet-holed from the Easter Rising, presides over one end of O'Connell Street. What has happened so often in the world since, in mass protests and civil rights demonstrations, was first patented in Ireland. The Irish were the first nation to recognise the potential of the popular movement for the goal of political reform. O'Connell led them first in a campaign for Catholic Emancipation, then in one for the repeal of the union between Britain and Ireland. This meant that the Irish people, downtrodden, illiterate and impoverished though many of them were, had a high level of political sophistication, and extremely effective mass organisations, long before they achieved their own sovereign political state.

Through clubs, newspapers, 'monster meetings' and the like, the indefatigable O'Connell, admiringly known as the Liberator, managed to involve an enormous number of the common people in his political campaigns. He finally forced a reluctant Britain into conceding the right of Catholics to sit in parliament, and was the first to do so himself. The so-called penal laws of the eighteenth century had deprived Irish Catholics of this privilege, along with a range of other restrictions on their citizenship. O'Connell accomplished all of this with a minimum of violence; he had killed a man in a duel in his early years, and trusted to the power of mass pressure rather than physical force. Flamboyant, devious, larger-than-life and a magnificent orator, this crafty old rogue was said to be the most popular politician of nineteenth-century Europe. He was accorded almost godlike status by his own people, and knew just how to humour and cajole them. He was also cordially detested by many of the British, which did him no harm at all in the eyes of his compatriots.

Later in the nineteenth century, this experiment in mass politics was to be repeated by the Protestant landowner Charles Stewart Parnell, whose statue adorns the other end of O'Connell Street. Aloof, reserved, English in manner and bafflingly enigmatic in his speech, Parnell was the temperamental opposite of O'Connell, but just as politically astute. He helped to found the Land League, which pressurised Irish landlords to reduce their rents, and became the greatest mass movement in the Europe of its day. Among other things, it bequeathed to history the word 'boycott', after a landlord's agent named Captain Charles Boycott who was given the cold shoulder by his irate tenants. Some cynics claim that this was because the Irish were unable to pronounce the word 'ostracism'. The impetus set up by the Land League was to result in the downfall of the Anglo-Irish landlords, whose lands were expropriated by the British state and sold to their tenants. But Parnell had his personal downfall too, as his adulterous relationship with a colleague's wife came to light and was used by his enemies to bring him low. On one occasion, when disturbed with the lady in question, he beat a retreat down a fire escape; and when his statue was erected in O'Connell Street, there was a suggestion that a fire escape should run down the back of it to ground level.

IRISH, THE

A mythical folk. There is no single bunch of people called the Irish. Instead there are Gaelic-Irish, Norman-Irish, Anglo-Irish, Scots-Irish, Danish-Irish and nowadays a sprinkling of Chinese-Irish too. Dubliners divide into Northsiders (the 'knackers' or working class who live north of the river Liffey), and Southsiders (the middle classes to the south of it). Northsiders are the sort of people you find in films like *The Commitments*, and are the subject of some scabrous jokes. ('How can you tell when a Northside girl has an orgasm?' 'She drops her chips.') The nation as a whole is made up of culchies and jackeens, yuppies and yokels, saints and Satanists, travellers and settled people, nationalists and anti-nationalists, heroin addicts and holy water addicts, mystical monks and atheistic intellectuals.

'Culchies' is the Dubliner's contemptuous word for all those Irish who are ill-starred enough not to live in the capital. Culchies are bumpkins, eejits (idiots), yokes (yokels), who eat their cabbage with a pitchfork and think pasta is a name for a priest. Culchies, in turn, regard Dublin as a seething sink of corruption which makes Gomorrah look like Goldilocks land, and suspect that the flashy, fornicating, tofu-eating jackeens (Dubliners) aren't truly Irish. (Though as some wag once remarked, we're all Irish in the eyes of God ...)

Then there are Cork people. Like God, Cork people are in a class of their own. Cork, a pleasant, hilly port on the south coast, is Ireland's second largest city, though only an eighth of the size of Dublin. Don't mention that to a Corkonian, however, or you'll be lucky to escape with your life. The natives of Cork have never heard of Dublin, let alone of Denver or Delhi. They believe themselves to be the only city on the planet, and behave as if they own it. The planet, that is, not the city. They're an idiosyncratic race of folk, with an accent which requires simultaneous translation through earphones. Cork people are seen by their critics as vainglorious boasters, and are seen by themselves as the finest bunch of people ever to grace God's earth. Both things might just be true.

It's a myth, by the way, that's there's something called an Irish accent. Kerry farmers don't speak at all like Dublin butchers, and the middle class don't speak like the working class. Anyone with a faintly indignant-sounding sing-song accent comes from Northern Ireland. There's a lot to be indignant about.

IRISH NATION

'A nation,' remarks a character in James Joyce's novel *Ulysses*, 'is the same people living in the same place.' Or in the case of Ireland, one might add, the same people trying to get out of the same place. No experience has been more native to Ireland than leaving it. For the last hundred or so years, the island has been emptying like a burning building, as the Irish have sailed off to try their luck elsewhere.

This makes for a strange situation. Whereas most nations are landmasses with people living on them, with Ireland the landmass is in one place and most of the people in another. If the geography of Ireland is in one spot, much of its history has happened elsewhere. One result of this is that the landmass itself becomes rapidly unreal. For a lot of its former inhabitants, or for their descendants, it has been transformed into a realm of mythical memory, an imaginary terrain which bears less and less resemblance to the physical reality. Ireland becomes a museum, a fantasy, a consoling fiction, a country of the mind. The country nostalgically recalled by a lot of emigrants, or even by those of Irish stock who have never clapped eyes on the place, is as much a phantom as Atlantis. Ireland becomes more like Camelot than Cambodia, a country where time has been magically suspended, a spiritual Disneyland which compensates for all that's absent from one's actual, dingy existence.

This, however, isn't the only reason why the Irish nation is a hard place to find. There's also the question of how many nations there are on the island. And being smart at arithmetic won't help you here. For an Irish Republican, there's just one Irish nation, part of which is currently occupied by an alien power known as the British. For some Republicans, there *seem* to be two different peoples on the island, with their different customs, accents, currencies and political institutions; but on this view those Northern Protestants who call themselves British are really Irish without knowing it. So the border between the two regions is real, but it's also in a sense illusory. Like the hapless woman whom the conjurer saws in half, the country is secretly one but appears to be in two bits. If and when a united Ireland arrives, the lady will step triumphantly forth to show that she's still in one piece.

For a Northern Unionist, on the other hand, there are one-and-a-bit countries on the island: the Irish Republic, and a province of Britain known as Northern Ireland. However, some Northern Irish Protestants regard themselves as being both British and Irish at the same time. And to complicate matters even further, some of them ('loyalists' rather than 'Unionists') see their primary allegiance as being to the ancient province of Ulster, part of which these days is actually in the Irish Republic. As if all that wasn't confusing enough, there are those in Ireland who hold that the answer to the Northern conflict is to convert one-and-a-bit nations into two. The idea is that Northern Ireland should become an autonomous state, independent of both Dublin and London.

On the whole, though, Belfast regards itself as much closer to Glasgow than to Dublin. For a Northern Unionist, the Republic of Ireland is as foreign a territory as Bulgaria, and has no more right than Bulgaria to meddle in its internal affairs. For some hard-line Unionists, the problem is that they have an alien wedge of people living amongst them known as the Irish, who are disloyal to the British state. A lot of Northern Catholics, by contrast, believe that they are on their own home ground, and that it is the Protestants who are the alien interlopers. Viewed from this standpoint, it's not hard to see why the question of Northern Ireland isn't going to be solved by a few smart ideas.

Like mercury, then, Irishness is a slippery thing to wrap one's fingers around. Quite a few people who live on the island don't regard themselves as Irish, while a lot of men and women who have never set foot in the place do. Others, as we've seen, see themselves as Irish and non-Irish at the same time. So is being Irish a matter of belonging to a state, or is it a state of mind? Is it cultural, or ethnic, or political, or territorial? Is it like being Belgian, or is it more like being a Buddhist? Are you Irish if you think you are?

And where exactly is the country to be located? Ireland is part of Europe, but it's a self-contained bit of it perched on the extreme western edge, with a larger island, Britain, blocking its view. (Though Britain is actually closer to France than it is to Ireland.) The Irish writer James Joyce scorned the country as 'an afterthought of Europe'. Ireland is part of what some maps call the 'Atlantic periphery', and scores fairly low on a scale of accessibility to European markets. London, on the other hand, is defined as part of the European 'core'. So is Edinburgh, even though it's as far from the heart of Europe as Dublin is. If you look at Ireland in terms of economic access, Dublin and Belfast rank with Warsaw, Lisbon and Bucharest as on the outer fringe of Europe, even though those cities are geographically speaking close to the heart of the European continent.

So Dublin is a lot nearer to London geographically than it is economically. It's physically quite close to Canterbury, but in many ways psychologically closer to Chicago. And it's certainly spiritually closer to Rome than it is to Reading. The ocean which cuts it off from New York is also a bridge across which millions have trooped to and fro. And how close is Ireland to Britain? You can actually see the British coastline from some spots on the island, but this is a bit deceptive. Before it won its independence, Ireland was part of the British Isles, but it was also an enormous way off from them. The two countries shared the same political sovereignty, but culturally speaking they were in some respects light-years apart. Ireland was too close to Britain to be ignored, but too different to be fully integrated. Like a confused, conflicting couple, the two nations could never quite decide whether they were going steady, divorced, blissfully wedded or locked into a shotgun marriage. They found it hard to figure out whether the obsessive fascination they felt for each other was undying love or visceral hatred.

If the Irish nation is hard to find, it isn't only because so much of it is abroad. It's also because these days 'abroad' has come to it, in the form of the transnational corporations which control so much of its economy. If Ireland gives such a hearty welcome to these 'immigrants', then it might also spare a thought for those newcomers to its shores who are seeking political asylum, or just a decent standard of living. In the Middle Ages, the Irish tended to stare through Britain to the rest of Europe, which is where they felt most at home. Ireland was an integral part of European Catholic Christianity, but also a place with its own highly distinctive culture. Its church, for example, never really saw itself as 'Roman' at all; it has its own quite separate traditions and identity. Monks, scholars and merchants moved back and forth between Ireland and the rest of Europe, just as business executives, rock groups and job-seeking young people whizz to and fro today. Since both Ireland and Britain are now members of the European Union, they can encounter each other in a more triangulated relationship, rather than being locked in eyeball-to-eyeball confrontation. The Union can play gooseberry, or marriage counsellor, between them.

But the Troubles in the North have also helped to shift Ireland's place on the global map. Some think that a healthy future for Northern Ireland means considering itself as a region of Europe, rather than just in relation to London and Dublin. And since the United States has been a key broker in seeking to resolve the political conflict, both parts of the island, like it or not, are now closer to Washington than they were before. The Troubles have put Ireland on the international map in ways that it could have done without. From Adelaide or Buenos Aires, Ireland means trouble. But internationalising the conflict in this way may also be a means of bringing it to an end.

JEWS

It's a myth that there are no Jews in Ireland. There have been Jews in the country since the early Middle Ages, when five of them were recorded as having visited the High King of Limerick. It's also recorded that they were sent back. Sephardic Jews came to Ireland when they were expelled from Spain and Portugal at the turn of the sixteenth century, and more arrived at the end of the nineteenth century as refugees from European pogroms. The Jewish community today numbers less than about two thousand, centred almost entirely in Dublin and Belfast.[18] Dublin has a fascinating Jewish museum which is well worth dropping in on, set in an area which used to be known as 'Little Jerusalem'.

One reason why there's so little anti-Jewish feeling in Ireland today is because in modern times the Irish never let them in. Shamefully, the Irish government during the darkest days of the Nazi persecution kept all but a few Jewish refugees from its shores.

There was an Irish fascist movement in the 1930s known as the Blueshirts, which was something of a Mickey Mouse outfit. Even so, anti-Semitic sentiment was widespread. There had been an anti-Jewish pogrom in the city of

---

[18] FIF: A former President of Israel, Chaim Herzog, was an Irishman.

Limerick around the turn of the century. Ireland was neutral in the Second World War, and wartime censorship banned reports of concentration camps and other Nazi atrocities. The idea was that such reports would inflame Irish public opinion and threaten the 'moral neutrality' of the state. The Irish Prime Minister of the day actually offered Germany his condolences on the death of Hitler, at the very time that news of the death camps was seeping out. Yet the Irish and the Jews have often been compared: they're both highly creative peoples scattered over the globe, and both are traditionally victims of racial prejudice. In fact one eighteenth-century scholar argued that the Irish *were* Jews. And the hero of the greatest Irish novel ever written, James Joyce's *Ulysses*, is a Dublin Jew.

In both cultures, the mother is a powerful emotional influence, strong and self-sacrificing. (How many Irish/Jewish mothers does it take to change a light bulb? None, I'll just sit here in the dark.) Jesus Christ, traditionally the most important man in Ireland, was also Jewish. How do we know? Because he lived with his mother for thirty years; he went into his father's business; his mother thought he was God; and he thought she was a virgin.

Visitors to Ireland, especially Americans, will be struck by the absence of black faces on the streets. It's not a multicultural society, since traditionally it was a place to get out of rather than escape to. Dublin is probably the least cosmopolitan of Europe's capital cities. One should remember too that if the Irish were colonised themselves, they also played an important role in the colonial mission of the British empire. A lot of them were involved in the slave trade, or became high-ranking colonial officials. Many Irish missionaries shared much the same supremacist mentality. As late as 1959, the Irish Prime Minister declared that his government entertained 'nothing but friendly sentiments for South Africa'. But the country is now on the brink of becoming more ethnically mixed, after a long hibernation; there are about 20,000 members of ethnic minorities in Northern Ireland alone.

The famous Irish reputation for hospitality is thus about to undergo its severest test. A kitschy Irish song speaks of a 'welcome on the mat', but the phrase rhymes with 'Timothy and Pat', not Abdul and Gargi. Will the Irish welcome strangers as they themselves were so often embraced by other nations, or will they hound and revile them, as they were so often vilified themselves? The omens, alas, are not at all good. Despite their contentiousness, the Irish are good on the whole at tolerating one another, since friendship tends to override differences of opinion. In a small nation, there's a feeling of all being in the same boat, whatever your conflicts. The Irish, surprisingly enough, are also good at tolerating strangers who bring them tangible benefits: tourists, transnational corporations, property speculators and fee-paying students. But Irish racism is steadily mounting, even before ethnic newcomers have entered the country in any significant numbers. The Irish State rigorously polices migration routes into the country, and discriminates against some immigrants and asylum seekers. Racial harassment has already hit the streets of Ireland, and some of the Irish are reacting to immigrants as they have traditionally reacted to their own 'tinkers' or travelling people (see TRAVELLERS), that's to say, with virulent hostility. It remains to be seen how skin-deep Irish warm-heartedness is. The Irish are still on the whole a genuinely hospitable crowd. But when it comes to foreign immigrants, some Irish eyes are smouldering rather than smiling.

JOYCE

One of Ireland's leading industries, involving T-shirts, summer schools, pub crawls and a huge amount of kitsch. Rumour has it that this all goes back to an Irish writer called James Joyce, but this is probably mythical and certainly irrelevant.

Here is an example of the mythical Joyce's writing:

'He addle liddle phifie Annie ugged the little craythur. Wither hayre in honds tuck up your part inher. Oftwhile babulous, mithre ahead, with goodly trowel in grasp...'

Some think Joyce was the greatest Irish writer, some think he was writing in Albanian, and others think he was dyslexic.

KELLS, BOOK OF

Not all it's cracked up to be. Some scholars consider it an example of decadent art. All those elaborate whorls and flourishes suggest an obsessive attention to the form of the writing, rather than to what's being said. In this convoluted design, the part is beginning to predominate over the whole. There's a kind of mad logic to the intricacy of much medieval Celtic art. But you will visit the Book of Kells during your stay as surely as you will visit the bathroom. Americans should note that in Ireland and Britain, bathrooms are, as the word declares, for taking baths in, so that to ask for the bathroom on a train or in a pub is a bit like asking for the swimming pool on the subway, or the library in a taxi. In Britain, ask for the lavatory or loo if you are upper-middle-class, the toilet if you are lower-middle-class, and the bog if you are one of the vulgar lower orders. Some of the British will try to persuade you that public lavatories there are red boxes on the street with slots in the top. Don't listen to them: they're just being mischievous, since these are actually mail boxes. Don't believe them either if they tell you that the English Tourist Board employs clowns who wander the streets in blue helmets and uniforms, waiting for tourists to knock their helmets off. They're just trying to get you arrested.

Likewise, ignore any smartass who tells you to shake hands effusively with all your fellow travellers when you climb into an English train compartment. Those visiting Britain should also remember that what you say, if you haven't heard what somebody says, depends on your social class. Say 'aye?' if you are working class, 'pardon?' if you are lower middle class, 'sorry?' if you are middle class, and 'what?' if you are upper class. Say nothing if you are the

Queen, since she doesn't have much small talk. The British are most particular about such things, and you are likely to be deported if you get them wrong.

KERRYMAN

Considered by Irish sophisticates everywhere to be a dim-witted, thick-skulled peasant. The butt of many jokes, such as: 'What's a Kerryman's foreplay?' Answer: 'Brace yerself, Bridget.' There is also the one about the Kerryman who moved to Cork and lowered the average IQ of both counties.

KILLARNEY

The fourth big disappointment of the holiday. This drab little town is infested by more tourists than almost anywhere else in Ireland – not because there's much worth seeing, but because it's the gateway to the lakes of Killarney, one of Ireland's loveliest regions. If you can get to the lakes by flinging yourself out of a helicopter, you'll save yourself a lot of discomfort.

LAND OF SAINTS AND SCHOLARS

Not entirely a myth, at least not at one period. In the so-called Dark Ages, when Europe was overrun by so-called barbarians, Ireland was one of the few centres of civilisation to be left intact. This was partly because its geographical remoteness kept it free from invasion. The Romans took one look at the place and decided it would be too costly to clean up the litter. The sixth to the eighth centuries in Ireland were a Golden Age of illuminated manuscripts, gorgeously decorated art and an intricate system of law. If it hadn't been for the Irish, the Latin language would probably have sunk without trace, which is one reason for school children to detest the Irish.

Irish culture at the time was immensely self-confident and open to cosmopolitan influence. Ireland was then the intellectual centre of Europe: its monasteries were celebrated for their learning, foreign scholars flocked to the island, and Irish monks sailed out to Europe as teachers and missionaries, as indeed they cover the globe with their missions today. An Irish priest today who is sent to, say, Birmingham in England might regard himself as a missionary. Some monks bore witness to their faith by setting sail in boats without food, water or any means of steering. This sometimes proved a remarkably convenient way of getting to heaven rather than to Europe.

Irish bards were extraordinarily powerful figures, a cross between poet, magician, lawyer and political counsellor. They could travel freely from one Irish kingdom to another, which was more than the kings themselves could do. Later there were wandering poets and harpists, some of them blind, who would shack up at a lord's castle, sing for their supper, and put a curse on the place if the food wasn't up to scratch. But this culture began to fail in the seventeenth century, once the Gaelic chieftains who supported it were driven out of the country into political exile.

No other nation of such modest size has produced such a magnificent race of writers. The Irish language has the oldest vernacular literature in Europe, one of stunning beauty and richness. It's true that there have been some slip-ups. In the eighteenth century, a learned scholar wrote a dictionary in Irish which managed to miss out the letter S. Things have been looking up in this century, however, when four

Irishman – Yeats, Shaw, Beckett and Heaney – have won the Nobel prize for literature.[19] Only France has bagged the prize more often. Literature in Ireland is now part of the tourist industry. There are scores of literary summer schools scattered throughout the country, which are said to divide into two kinds: those in which you drink between the lectures, and those in which you lecture between the drinks. If someone in Ireland jotted down an atrocious limerick on the back of an envelope in 1893, you can be sure there's now an annual summer school on him.

A lot of the great names of 'English' literature were actually Irish, though they sometimes forgot the fact. The English adopt the Irish when it suits them, and dump them when it doesn't. When the Irish actor Richard Harris won an award for his part in a British film, the English newspapers headlined the story: 'English actor wins award'. When he was arrested for disorderly conduct in a bar, the headline ran: 'Irish actor in bar brawl'. Another Irish actor, Peter O'Toole, has been nominated for more academy awards than anyone else, but has won none of them. This endears him to the Irish, since they get uneasy when people, especially Irish people, enjoy too much success. There's a tradition in the country of regarding high achievers as suffering from some rare mental disorder.

The English tend to think of Irish writers as permanently out of their skulls on Guinness and whiskey, which is yet another myth. Apart from a few flamboyant exceptions, Irish authors have been far less alcoholic than American ones. In fact it's hard to think of a well-known American writer who

---

[19] FIF: The Irish buy more volumes of poetry per head than any other English-speaking people.

was sober for any significant stretch of time. Irish writers watch each other warily to see which of them will be taken up by a prestigious London publishing house. Colonialism still lives on in cultural affairs. Today, Irish artists of all kinds pay no income tax, which in a country where income tax can amount to a hefty slice of your earnings is the best incentive ever dreamt up for growing your hair long and buying yourself a pen or a paintbrush. Not many of the Irish are millionaires, but some of them are taxed as though they were. An elected group of artists receive bursaries from the state and form a society modelled on the ancient bards. Ireland is stuffed with poets, literary journals and theatre companies, boasts a flourishing film industry, and some of

the finest traditional music in the world. It is confidently expected that exemption from income tax will shortly be extended to saints as well.

You occasionally run across ordinary, non-intellectual people in Ireland who have read some Joyce, Yeats or Heaney. Even if they haven't read them, they will certainly have heard of them, whereas the ordinary English person is unlikely to have heard of T.S. Eliot. A friend of mine once encountered a Dublin taxi-driver who raved on about the great Irish writer Orson Wells. He probably meant Oscar Wilde, though oddly enough the young Orson Wells did learn his acting trade in Ireland. The story is told of an Irish worker on an English building site who was being bawled out by the foreman. 'Why, you thick Paddy,' he snarled, 'You wouldn't even know the difference between a joist and a girder.' 'Sure I do,' said the Irishman. 'Joyce wrote *Ulysses* and Goethe wrote *Faust*.'

Irish intellectuals are an eloquent, quarrelsome bunch who talk non-stop about themselves and their country.[20] The Irish are endlessly fascinated by themselves, which among other things is the mark of a small, parochial nation. That's why some of them are reading this book right now. French or English intellectuals don't talk much about being French or English because they don't need to. It's only a marginal people who have an identity problem, and so keep examining themselves all the time.

Not long ago, Ireland had a well-known intellectual as its Prime Minister. When policy proposals were put before him, he is reputed to have said: 'That's all very well in practice,

---

[20] FIF: Though they sometimes talk about other things too. The word 'electron' was coined by an Irish scientist.

but will it work in theory?' But though Irish intellectuals are a group apart, as anywhere else in the world, many of them are closer to the ground than their British counterparts. Some of them may only be a generation or two away from the farm. Ireland has more of a common culture than England, though there are some sharp gradations within it. There's a distinguished Trinity College professor who even advertises cars on television, though it's common knowledge that he doesn't drive. There's less snobbery among the Irish than in England, though the country has some socially exclusive circles too: the racing fraternity, the big business folk, the film stars, and the socialites of the old Anglo-Irish aristocracy. Anyone called Guinness is unlikely to be found propping up the bar in pubs where they sell the product. In fact, one or two of this aristocratic family can't stand the sight of the stuff. Which brings us to ...

LIFFEY WATER

The Liffey is Dublin's main river, and its water is thought to be the magical ingredient in brewing Guinness. Irish Guinness is sometimes thought to be superior to London-brewed Guinness for just this reason. One is pained to report that this is yet another myth. The Liffey was never the source of the water used in the brewing. Anyone who has taken a peep at the Liffey will be mightily relieved to hear it.

LIMERICK

Do limericks come from Limerick? Nobody knows, but probably not. The verse known as a limerick has a long history and no obvious connection with the Irish city of that name. One theory is that people used to sit round inventing limericks on the spot, and to give each person time to think, the others recited an old song which goes 'Oh won't you come up, come all the way up, come all the way up to Limerick?' There is no truth in the rumour that there is also a verse-form known as a 'Cork', an endless epic poem which consists entirely of bragging. There is, however, a verse-form known as a Skibbereen, which was invented by one of the greatest living Irish wits, the Gaelic scholar Seán Mac Réamoinn. (Skibbereen is a small town in County Cork, notorious for its suffering during the Great Famine.) This consists of two rhyming lines, the first of which you make up yourself, the second of which is a line from an old Irish song: 'And that's another reason I left old Skibbereen.' For example: 'They taught me smooching was a sin and *Ulysses* obscene, And that's another reason I left old Skibbereen.' Over to you. There's also a verse known as the Listowel, which is halfway between a limerick and a skibbereen. This is because the small Kerry town of Listowel is between them too.

The town of Limerick lies on the estuary of the River Shannon, the longest river in either Ireland or Britain. Its basin covers over a fifth of the entire country. The poet Robert Graves once said that everyone died of drink in Limerick except for the Plymouth Brethren, who died of religious melancholia. Nobody knows whether this is true, but probably not.

MARKIEVICZ, CONSTANCE

One of the greatest of all Irish rebels. Born in Sligo to wealthy parents, Connie Markievicz joined the Irish nationalist movement late last century, became a member of the executive council of Sinn Fein, and wrote articles for the first woman's newspaper in Irish history. She also founded and drilled the nationalist youth movement, which was a kind of revolutionary equivalent of the Boy Scouts. Armed to the teeth herself, she was said to be easy to mistake for the sales representative of a firm of small arms manufacturers. A convinced socialist, she played a leading part in setting up soup kitchens to feed the starving Dublin poor during an industrial conflict in 1913. She also married a flamboyant Polish Count and, much to his dismay, turned his house into a kind of revolutionary commune.

Markievicz became a Major in the Irish Citizen Army, designed her own female version of its uniform, and saw active service in the Easter Rising of 1916. She was condemned to death by the British, a sentence she apparently greeted with delight, but was reprieved because of her sex and endured the first of several spells of imprisonment. In 1918 she became Labour spokeswoman in the first (officially illegal) Sinn Fein government. She prevented some vital state papers from falling into the hands of the British authorities by driving them around Dublin in a taxi and then depositing them in the window of an antique shop, protected by a prohibitively high price tag. The shop was right opposite the headquarters of the Black and Tans, the motley crew of thugs recruited by the British government to help put down the Irish during the war of independence. As Labour Minister she intervened on the side of the workers in a number of industrial disputes, including one at a rosary bead factory.

While imprisoned in London's Holloway gaol, Markievicz was elected to parliament as Britain's first ever female Member. As a good Republican, however, she refused to take up her seat. She was imprisoned yet again, got herself court-martialled for conspiracy, and went on the run during the civil war which followed Irish independence. She was finally slung in jail yet again, this time not by the British but by the very Irish Free State she had helped to bring into being.

Markievicz continued her campaigning among the destitute of Dublin, snatched time to run a theatre company, and died in 1927. The Irish government refused to allow her body to lie in state. Shunned by her upper-class friends, and beaten up more than once by the police, she abandoned her money and well-heeled background in the cause of radical republicanism, and helped to keep a hungry working class alive. It was their love, along with little else, that she carried to her grave.

MATCH-MAKING

In traditional Ireland, marriages were often arranged by a professional matchmaker. Often enough, you got married to avoid having to emigrate, enter a convent or become a priest. You might also marry to get your hands on a dowry, take over your father's farm, and have a plentiful supply of mini-labourers known as children to help you work it. Match-makers were on hand at fairs and social gatherings to manage the whole affair, to negotiate between the two families, and to use their legal knowledge to draw up a contract. The whole business wasn't all that different from selling a pig. And if the contract turned out to be a bad one, you were stuck with it for life, in a land without divorce. The town of Lisdoonvarna in County Clare, which is, alas, nothing like as beautiful as its name, ran a thriving marriage market. At the end of the harvest, bachelor farmers would move into the town's hotels, young unmarried women would flock to join them, and a good many marital bargains were successfully struck. Some of this still goes on in Lisdoonvarna today. *You* may be romantic about the Irish, but they were rarely romantic about each other.

MILESIUS

Legendary king who founded the Irish race. Luckily for him he didn't exist, since he has a great deal to answer for.

MYSTERIES

There have been three fundamental mysteries in Ireland. The first is why there is nothing of any significance beginning with the letter Q (see Q). The second is why the Virgin Mary chose to make an appearance at an inconvenient, out-in-the-sticks place like the village of Knock, rather than attract more publicity and credibility by landing in one of Dublin's sports stadiums during an international match. The third mystery has been the source of the considerable personal wealth of Charles Haughey, former Prime Minister and leader of *Fianna Fáil*. Otherwise known as the Boss or the Great National Bastard, Haughey has enjoyed a luxurious life-style, including a mansion near Dublin and his own private island off the Irish coast, while doing a passable impersonation of a Plain Man of the People. All things to all persons, Haughey was Gaelic chieftain, hard-living rogue and hard-nosed operator rolled into one, both crafty pragmatist and custodian of the sacred nationalist flame. He has now acknowledged that he accepted some hand-outs from a prominent Irish businessman, though the public wringing of hands over this confession is yet another example of the gap in Irish culture between what's officially supposed to happen and what everyone knows actually happens. It was a bit like being horrified to discover that Madonna isn't a virgin.

MUSIC

To claim that you can stroll into a back street Irish pub, or a pub way out in the wilds, and stumble on spontaneous sessions of wonderful music, sounds like a myth. On the whole, it isn't. You can come across champion performers almost anywhere. One reason for this is that almost every Irish musician is hyped as a champion.

Traditional Irish music lives on partly because it takes easily to being blended with more up-to-date stuff. The Irish music scene has produced some wonderfully creative combinations of traditional music with rock, punk, classical, cajun, native American and the like.[21] One of the most alluring sounds in the country, apart from 'I'm paying for the drinks', is that of a woman singing unaccompanied in the native language. In this 'sean-nos' (old-style) form of song, the voice is used more as an impersonal instrument than as an expression of individual personality. You let the tradition sing through you rather than aim for originality, and keep personal emotion to the minimum. Irish musicians dislike flashy self-presentation, and some fiddlers have been known to play with their backs to the audience. Even if Irish musicians have an audience, they sometimes tend to behave as though they're not there.

---

[21] FIF: Handel wrote much of the Messiah in Dublin, and the city witnessed its first performance in 1742.

A lot of Irish music comes to us only from the oral tradition, collected and written down by scholars who roamed the countryside in search of tuneful old codgers. One such expert asked an old woman where she had found a particular song, to be told that she had heard it sung by a blind harper from a village over the mountain. And where had he got it from? inquired the expert. From his old uncle, she replied, who had been a roving tinker. And where had he got it from? He got it from the radio.

In fact, there's a serious point behind the joke. A lot of what people regard as traditional Irish songs aren't traditional at all, and some of them aren't even Irish in origin. The words of 'Danny Boy' weren't written by an Irish composer. Genuine Irish singers and musicians wouldn't be found dead performing the sentimental drivel which some visitors think of as typically Irish.

Another story is told in Ireland of three fiddlers at a musical festival. The first stepped up wearing an expensive black suit and carrying a Stradivarius violin in a richly ornamented case made of Florentine leather. He took the violin out with exquisitely manicured fingers, placed it under his chin with a flourish, and drew the bow across it. And by God he was useless.

Then up stepped a second fiddler, a bit of a Flash Harry in a sequined suit and spotted bow tie, carrying a well-polished, moderately expensive fiddle. He placed it under his chin, swept back his oiled locks, bared his teeth to the audience in an glittering smile and began to play. And by God he was useless.

A third fiddler then shuffled to the front: a bent, wheezing little fellow in a beer-stained jacket with matchstick-thin legs and his behind hanging out of his trousers. He had no violin case, just a battered old instrument he had played since he was a lad. By this time the audience had lost patience and was barely listening. But the little old man fixed the fiddle under his grizzled chin with a shaking hand, and began slowly, tenderly, to play.

And by God he was useless too.

NEWGRANGE

Part of a cemetery of Stone Age kings about 30 miles north of Dublin, and one of the great neolithic sites of Europe. It is older than both Stonehenge and the Pyramids. The name, which sounds incongruously like a village in Surrey, in fact means 'the cave of Grainne', who was an ancient Irish heroine. There is a great circle of standing stones, and a passage which leads through 62 feet to the central burial chamber. The chamber itself, almost 5,000 years old, is over 19 feet high and superbly decorated with abstract art by its builders. We know almost nothing about them, except that they may have come to Ireland from France in the third millennium BC. Perhaps they believed that being buried here, at what for them might have been the very centre of the earth, would ensure a speedy transition to rebirth.

At sunrise on the winter solstice, the sun's rays infiltrate the chamber and illuminate it for about 17 minutes. Unless this is an accident, it must have taken some complex calculations, which as far as we know were made without computers. Though a small fossilised object has been unearthed which might just possibly be a neolithic mouse.

NO

There is no word in the Irish language for 'no', as you may have noticed when you ask the Irish if they'd like a drink. But then there's no word for 'yes' either. This is why, if you ask the Irish whether they are married or have a job, they tend to say 'I am' and 'I do' rather than 'yes'. Many speech habits in Irish-English (officially known as Hiberno-English) are carried over from the Irish language. 'Are you after having your dinner?' meaning 'Have you had your dinner?', would be one such instance. Irish-English occasionally uses phrases that sound rather quaint to a foreigner, such as 'contagious to' for 'near'. Some scholars think that this comes from the Irish having originally learned English from text books rather than from hearing it actually spoken. Think of how school Latin might sound to an ancient Roman.

One reason why the English have regarded the Irish as stupid is because they sometimes use the language differently. (Another reason is that you have to see your colonial subjects as dirty, lazy and thick-headed, otherwise it's hard to justify stealing their land and occupying their country.) A language is a way of thinking as well as a means of communication, and the Irish have had to adapt English to their own rather different thought patterns and cultural habits. What's known as an Irish bull is a remark which supposedly illustrates the illogicality of the Irish from an English standpoint. You ask an Irishman in the street the way to the bank, and myth has it that he replies 'Well now, I wouldn't start from here'. In fact, so-called Irish bulls are just the mark of a different pattern of thought. In losing their own language, the Irish have tragically lost touch with a great many of their spiritual resources, and with much of their unique identity.

Some people in the Irish Republic think mistakenly that in Northern Ireland, 'no' is the *only* word ever used. This is because Northern Unionists have been notorious for rejecting any scheme for changing the political status quo. In response to one such plan, the Belfast city hall hung out a huge banner reading 'Ulster Says No'. It was fairly near Christmas, and someone suggested that by adding 'el' to the end, they could save themselves the cost of a Christmas message. Which brings us to ...

NORTHERN IRELAND

The hottest Irish potato of all. Even calling it Northern Ireland is politically debatable. Unionists would be happy enough with this name, but nationalists would prefer something like 'the six counties'. Don't talk to Unionists about 'Britain and Northern Ireland', since for them Northern Ireland *is* part of Britain. Similarly, don't talk to Irish nationalists about the 'mainland', meaning Britain, since for them Ireland *is* the mainland. In fact there's nothing you can say on this topic which won't instantly alienate a few million people. So here goes.

Northern Ireland is not the same as Ulster. Ulster is one of the four provinces of Ireland, and three of its counties are part of the Irish Republic. The other six counties of Ulster make up Northern Ireland, which is officially part of the United Kingdom and has been governed for some time from London. This region is the one part of Ireland in which Protestants form the majority. Unionists are those who want to keep it this way by retaining the British connection, whereas nationalists are those who want these six counties to be integrated into the largely Catholic Republic of Ireland. This means getting the British to pull out of the North, abolishing the border, doing away with Northern Ireland as it exists, and creating instead a united Ireland. Most nationalists want to do this by peaceful, constitutional means; a minority of them want to force it through by violence. The best-known of these are the IRA, better known in the North as the Provos.

Let's take the nationalist view first. Nationalists think that the British have no right to be in Ireland because it isn't their country. In their eyes, the whole existence of Northern Ireland is a hangover from an outdated British imperialism. For them, the British presence in the North is as scandalous as if Britain still occupied Canada or India. Northern Ireland, they argue, is an artificial state which was created at the time of Irish independence so that the Protestants (known derisively by some as 'snouts') in the North could safeguard their political and economic privileges. They didn't want to join the more impoverished south of Ireland, thus losing the benefits which being British subjects could bring them. And some of them betray an unpleasantly supremacist attitude to Catholics as a bunch of benighted bogtrotters.

The borders of Northern Ireland were deliberately rigged so that Protestants would outnumber Catholics, and thus be able to lord it over them. Northern Ireland became a kind of apartheid state, in which the sizeable Catholic minority were treated as second-class citizens, discriminated against in housing, unemployment and a variety of other ways. Irish Catholics were turned into strangers in their own land, forced to live under a British rule many of them abhorred. Their cultural identity was denied them; and when they began to protest against all this in the late 1960s, the result was a Protestant backlash, the despatching of British troops to the North, the re-emergence of the IRA, and the shootings and bombings which lasted for more than a quarter of a century. The Unionists maintain that they want to continue being British, but for Irish nationalists that's just a coded way of saying that they want to go on exercising power over the Northern Catholics.

What is the Unionist view of this? The Unionists are Protestants of mainly British stock, who were settled in Ireland by the British in the seventeenth century. Irish land was confiscated and granted to them instead, while a lot of the native Irish were driven onto poorer soil. So the Northern Protestants arrived in the country as colonial settlers. But this, so Unionists would argue, was all a long time ago. If you can't claim a right to live in a place after three centuries of continuous settlement, however you came to be there in the first place, it's a poor prospect. On this logic, the Americans should go back to wherever they came from, and the Irish themselves should restore the country to whoever was living there when they first arrived, if they happen to be still around, which in fact they aren't.[22]

Some Unionists will admit that they have treated the Catholic minority shabbily, though some will not. Catholics for some of them are 'Teagues' or 'Fenian bastards'. Even so, the Protestants argue, they themselves are a distinctive people, and have the right to preserve their own culture and govern themselves. What goes for the Catholic nationalists goes for them too. They won't be coerced by violence into joining what they regard as a foreign nation, the Irish

---

[22] FIF: The inhabitants of Ireland before the Celts arrived, a few centuries before the birth of Christ, are known as firbolgs, which means 'bagmen' in Irish. Myth has it that they carried around earth with magical properties in leather bags. The male part of the race died out, but the females, known as bag ladies, have survived.

Republic, in which their Protestant culture and identity would risk being obliterated.

What is the Irish Republic's perspective on all this? Very few of its citizens support the IRA, though a lot of them are nationalists in some broader, vaguer sense of the word. Many of them would eventually like to see a united Ireland, even though this might mean Dublin having to foot the bill for the North, an economically ailing region which the Republic couldn't easily afford.[23] And some people in the Republic aren't greatly enthused by the prospect of having a million disgruntled Protestants dumped on them. One reason why the Irish Republic has been relatively free of internal conflict is that the creation of Northern Ireland meant that it 'exported' some of its problems over the border. Because of that border, the Republic is an artificially cohesive society.

In any case, Northern Ireland comes dismally low down on the Republic's list of priorities. People there are far more concerned about the cost of living, or about health and education, than they are about the plight of their co-religionists in the North. Many in the Republic have tried to turn their back on the problem, seeing it as an embarrassing obstacle to their own attempts to modernise. For one thing, it scares foreign capital away from Ireland; for another thing it gets the Irish an international reputation as a lot of sectarian crazies who are still living in the seventeenth century. At the same time, the Dublin government has played a key role in the peace negotiations, even though Unionists resent this as the interference of a foreign power in Northern Ireland's affairs.

---

[23] FIF: The British government spends over £3 billion a year to keep Northern Ireland economically afloat, about a third of the province's total income.

Finally, the view from across the water. A slim majority of the British would like to see their troops and government pull out of Northern Ireland. Though the Unionists regard themselves as British, many of the 'mainland' British don't really agree. A lot of them see Northern Ireland as a pain in the neck and would be glad to be rid of it. Why not just pull out Our Boys and let the feckless Micks fight it out among themselves? The British government, on the other hand, fears the political danger of appearing to give way to terrorism, and feels that it has responsibilities to the Unionists – though it has also declared that it has no selfish interest in remaining in Ireland, which doesn't please the Unionists a bit. The future of the North, say the British, is up to the Irish people themselves. The question is, up to which of the Irish people? The Unionists claim that they themselves should decide what happens to them; the nationalists say that the decision should lie with the Irish people as a whole, both north and south of the border.

There's no shortage of solutions to the problem, at least on paper. You could abolish the border and create a united Ireland, guaranteeing the Northern Protestants their civil and cultural rights within it. You could even grant them self-government within a federal Ireland. The only problem with this is that some Unionists wouldn't believe the Dublin government if it announced that rain was wet, let alone if it assured them that it would respect their rights. Though in fact there's arguably no reason why the Republic should persecute the Protestants if they were to join it. The Irish Republic is rapidly becoming a secular, pluralist, more liberal-minded place, which means that the Northern Protestants would have less to fear from becoming part of it. They wouldn't find themselves deprived of divorce and contraception, as they would have done some years ago, though some might find themselves with a lower standard of living. A lot of Northern Protestants are deeply alarmed at the prospect of coming under the sway of the Catholic Church, and have some reason for this fear. But the power of the Catholic Church is taking an almighty battering in the Republic these days. Alternatively, you could maintain the present division of the island, but give the Catholics in the North more rights and power. Some of this has already been tried, but it won't satisfy many nationalists, and many Unionists look upon greater Catholic power in the North as the thin end of the Catholic Ireland wedge. (Or, as one Northern Protestant preacher luridly put it, 'the thin end of the Scarlet Woman'.) Then again, you could try what's known as joint sovereignty, in which Britain and the Irish Republic would both be in charge of the North. But neither Unionists or nationalists will currently buy this. Alternatively, you could have an independent Northern Ireland, ruled neither by London or Dublin, which might fit well enough with the European Community's policy of greater regional autonomy. But it isn't clear, among other difficulties, that this would be economically viable.

A new agreement has now been struck, under which Northern Ireland will have its own democratic assembly, and there will be institutional links between both parts of the island and between Ireland and Britain. A more practical solution would be to punch a perforated line where the border is now, tear off everything to the top of it, and float it out to sea. If *you* have a solution to the crisis, write it instantly on a postcard and send it to 'Northern Ireland: The Answer', c/o the publishers of this book. The author of the most inventive solution will win a holiday for two in Tallaght, one of the country's most celebrated beauty spots.

Northern Ireland, however, is a lot more than sectarian strife. It is one of the most attractive areas of Ireland, with superb scenery, a magnificent coastline and warm, trustworthy, considerate people. Its proudly Protestant culture is complex, deep-rooted and full of fascination. For obvious reasons the place pulls in too few tourists these days, which is exactly why you should visit it. You are far more likely to get shot in Washington or Capetown.

O

A remarkably common blood group in Ireland, especially in the west and north. Its distribution in Europe is markedly peripheral, occurring as it does in Scotland, Iceland, the Basque country and the western Mediterranean. The Aran islanders, however, have a high proportion of blood group A, which some think comes from consorting a bit too freely with Cromwellian soldiers. No less than 80% of the Irish are said to have lightly pigmented eyes. This is not the kind of fact likely to prove of vital use to tourists, but it might always serve you as an opening gambit in a nightclub.

OIRISH

How the Irish are supposed to pronounce 'Irish'. Mostly a myth. The word also means any self-conscious display of Irishness, such as wearing a green hat and falling around the place saying 'Bejasus'. Parading your Irishness is infrequent in Ireland, since the Irish don't usually go around thinking of themselves as Irish any more than turkeys go around thinking of themselves as turkeys. But if it happens at all, it's probably for your benefit. You may run into the odd Irish person who needs somebody to be Irish at. Remember that a lot of things in the country would be different if you, the tourist, weren't there. For one thing, there wouldn't be any thatched cottages which were built in 1989 but are feebly trying to look as though they've been there since the Vikings invaded.

The Irish are understandably sensitive to being stereotyped as Oirish, given that they've been branded in their time as apes, thugs, drunks, brawlers, liars, idlers, braggarts, clowns, thickheads, children, and women. And that includes the men. On the other hand, a lot of the Irish don't mind if you stereotype them as charming, eloquent, witty and imaginative. So stereotype away if you must, but make it complimentary.

O'MALLEY, GRACE

A wicked Irishwoman. She was a rebel against Queen Elizabeth I in the sixteenth century, and for forty years was the moving spirit behind anti-English uprisings in the west of the country. She commanded a large private army, a fleet of boats, and was a formidable military strategist. Through her kinsfolk and allies, Grace dominated most of the fortresses of the western seaboard. In fact she was a notorious pirate, sailing up and down the western coast and giving the English a hard time. She had her eye on a fine castle, and secured it by marrying its owner on a trial basis for a year. At the end of the year she kicked him out, having taken care to get pregnant by him in the meanwhile to secure herself an heir.

Then she went to war with the English again, but suffered some losses and came to an agreement with Queen Elizabeth, who she went to visit in London. If Grace had lived in the Ireland of the 1930s, or even the 1950s, she would have been ordered to stay at home and polish the drawbridge.

PATRICK

Patron saint of Ireland. As such, he has the following drawbacks:

1. We don't really know who he was.
2. We don't really know where he came from.
3. He wasn't the first Christian missionary to Ireland.
4. There may have been two of him.
5. He may not have existed at all.

Apart from that, he's a grand sort of patron saint entirely. He probably came to Ireland as a slave, and he was the first individual in recorded history to write against slavery. He is also said to have driven all the snakes out of Ireland. Some people suggest that they ended up in Chicago city hall.

Several sacred places in Ireland have a special association with St. Patrick. One of them is Lough Derg in County Donegal, where the saint is said to have fasted and expelled evil spirits on Station Island in the lake. In the Middle Ages, men of high rank came to visit the spot from all over Europe; it may even be that Dante's great poem *The Divine Comedy* was influenced by it. The pilgrimage, known as St Patrick's Purgatory, still flourishes each year from June to August. It lasts for three days, on each of which only one meal, of dry bread and black tea, is permitted. Pilgrims must go barefoot, perform certain austere penances, and spend their first night without sleep in the island's church. Despite its extreme rigours, all sorts of ordinary Irish people regularly complete the pilgrimage. Other pilgrims climb Ireland's holy mountain, Croagh Patrick in Mayo, some of them barefoot. The Irish may be experts at enjoying themselves, but they're also professionals at self-denial.

PHOENIX PARK

Not only the biggest park in Ireland, but at almost 1,800 acres one of the grandest in Europe. The name 'Phoenix' has nothing to do with the mythological bird: it's a mistranslation of an Irish phrase meaning 'clear water', referring to a spring within the park. The park contains a zoo, the mansion of the President of Ireland, the residence of the US ambassador, a hospital, and a memorial to the Duke of Wellington, the biggest monument in Europe.

Wellington was an Irishman, but like many an Irishman who made good in England he pretended that he wasn't. His patriotic comment on being born in Ireland was that being born in a stable doesn't make you a horse. The Dubliner Oscar Wilde came to England as an Oxford student and threw away his Irish accent along with his boat ticket. Winston Churchill's private secretary was Irish; in fact his father was a Fenian revolutionary, though nobody could have guessed it. Irish people who ape the English used to be known as 'shoneens' or 'Castle Catholics', i.e. Catholics who scandalously accepted social invitations to Dublin Castle, which in colonial days was the headquarters of British authority in Ireland.

One traditional Irish attitude to the English has been a mixture of outward deference and secret resentment. But Ireland's role in the European Community is turning it gradually outward from its love/hate relationship with the British. Today it looks to Brussels, Paris and Berlin rather than just to London. In fact if the sea was lowered only 300 feet, Ireland would be part of the European mainland. It's a more self-confident, cosmopolitan place these days, just as it was in its medieval hey-day, though this can be exaggerated. The Irish still know a lot more about the English than they do about the Austrians, and are probably even worse than the English in picking up foreign languages. The place is still in some ways a closed, exclusive society. But small nations are more likely to be internationally-minded than large ones, since they can't survive without gazing beyond their own shores. Americans are famous for their shaky geography, which is why they say things like 'Paris, France', just in case you thought Paris was in Thailand.

The British, too, are in some ways more parochial than the Irish, and much more suspicious of the Europeans.

(Don't remind them that they *are* Europeans, since a lot of them don't want to know.) This is partly because the main contact they used to have with other nations was colonising them, which isn't the most effective way of getting to know them. Having lost their empire, they now sometimes find it difficult to relate to other peoples on equal terms. The Irish, by contrast, are now doing this for the first time in their recent history, and are proving rather good at it, as skilful negotiators within the European Union. None of this has anything to do with Phoenix Park, but Irish thinking is famously digressive.

PIGGY BANKS

Pigs have ranked among the most important members of the Irish nation. Physical contact with a pig, as with a donkey, was traditionally seen as a cure for various human ailments. It is rumoured that there are parts of the country where this physical contact was sometimes carried a little too far.

For the poor farmers, pigs operated as a kind of savings bank. You fed the creatures with potatoes as you might place money in the bank, and then you 'withdrew' these savings by selling the pigs when times were rough. A pig was a magical machine for converting potatoes into money, a kind of grunting, slobbering insurance policy. Unlike farm animals which can be milked, shorn or relieved of their eggs, the pig (the only farm animal native to Ireland, by the way) is fed only to be slaughtered. It's a grim enough life, without one's name becoming a by-word for filth into the bargain.

Like other domestic animals, the pig often shared the family cabin, snouting around in a corner of the living room. The Irish writer Flann O'Brien tells the tale of a government inspector who descended upon one such pig-infested cabin, and insisted that the family separate themselves from their animals by building a special shed attached to the house. When he returned to check up on them in a year's time, the pig was still in the house, and the shed was built but empty. Asked why this was so, the family replied that they had tried living in the shed for a bit, but had found it terribly cold.

POLITICS

Ireland has a President, which is a largely ceremonial function; a Prime Minister or *Taoiseach*; and a parliament or House of Congress known as the *Dáil* (pronounced Doil). The two main political parties are *Fianna Fáil* (prounced Fee-anna Foil) and *Fine Gael* (Feena Gael). Like a lot of rival political parties these days, they are sometimes hard to tell apart. Both of them date back to the civil war earlier this century over the Anglo-Irish Treaty of 1921. *Fianna Fáil* opposed the treaty, while *Fine Gael* supported it. *Fianna Fáil*, by far the largest party in the Republic with around 40% of the vote, is traditionally the party of small farmers and the urban working class. It is populist, morally traditionalist and (at least for its opponents) full of tribalism, religious piety and outdated nationalist sentiment. *Fine Gael* appeals more to the shopkeeping, professional and big business classes. Both parties could be described as centre-right. There's also a Labour Party, which is the oldest political party in the country, but which like most Labour Parties these days has ditched its socialist policies. And there are one or two smaller parties to both right and left.

Irish politics have been dominated by the 'national' issue to the exclusion of other questions. In an overwhelmingly rural country, for example, there's today no official farmers' party, as there is, say, in Norway. Much more than in Britain, politics cuts across social class: one of *Fianna Fáil*'s strengths has been its ability to draw support from all social classes. Personalities have traditionally counted for more than ideology. Because of the Irish system of electoral representation, parties which are supposed to be at loggerheads may find themselves in government together, which discourages too much doctrinal conflict.

The other reason why Irish politics aren't too bothered with beliefs is that Irish politicians have traditionally been more local fixers than national statesmen or women. The idea is that you give your vote to your local TD (Congressman or Member of Parliament), and in return for this favour the TD will make sure that that pot-holed bit of road outside your front door gets repaired. In an over-centralised country, this is sometimes the only way to get things done. TDs have to spend a lot of their time wooing their electorate, turning up at their dances and remembering the names of their seven children, and this tends to limit their political role. As with many things in Ireland, politics is a more chummy affair than it is elsewhere in Europe. The downside of this is corruption, which over the past few years has been rampant in Irish political life. Countries which place a high value on family life are likely to end up with political mafias.

Even so, so-called localism in Irish political life can be exaggerated. Evidence suggests that the Irish, like other advanced nations, nowadays think in national terms as much as in local ones. They also have a rather more robust faith in their public institutions than most other European nations, which some may think is no thanks to the institutions themselves.

Much of Ireland's political record this century has been pretty dismal. The country has been marked by economic stagnation, political isolationism, and a failure to exploit its resources for the benefit of the whole people. Having crawled out from beneath the paw of the British lion, it never really established its own distinctive institutions. What signs of nationhood it displayed were often fairly token: the Irish language, for instance, was reduced to a kind of ceremonial affair. Nor could governments bring a halt to mass emigration. To the deep embarrassment of the Irish state, more people left the country in the economically depressed 1950s than they did in the last quarter of a century of British rule.

Yet the problems the nation faced were immense. It was the first post-colonial country of the twentieth century, with no real model to guide it in the process of trying to forge for itself a new identity. British rule had bequeathed it – along with some more enlightened features – a history of poverty, economic backwardness, political oppression and low self-esteem, along with some ferocious sectarian conflicts. It was a small, claustrophobic offshore island with a rancorous history and little experience of modern-day citizenship. The country had never really had a political state of its own: traditional Gaelic society was divided up into a host of minor kingdoms, and when a centralised state finally arrived it was in the shape of imperial occupation. There was little tradition of civic responsibility, which some think accounts for all that spitting and littering. And it was a nation deeply scarred by the psychic wounds of famine, mass emigration and a chronic lack of self-confidence.

Given all this, it's a tribute to the Irish that their country during this century has been relatively peaceful, stable and democratic. It hasn't been marked by the despotism, political extremism or spectacular corruption of so many other post-colonial nations, and has sustained something like a political consensus, however stifling and stagnant. The statesman who steered it through the early decades of independence – Eamon de Valera – may have been a backward-looking, inward-looking autocrat, but he was no Hitler or Mussolini. And the Catholic Church, with its strong commitment to authority and the family, has been a force for stability as well as for an oppressive conservatism.

In any case, Ireland managed to side step some of the conflicts which have besieged other modern states. Given its de-industrialised economy, along with the importance of the national question, class politics never really took firm root. National unity was possible partly because one force which threatened it – the Protestant North – had been cordoned off by a political frontier. The Irish Republic may not have desired this, but in some ways it has profited from it. The country managed for a long time to avoid some of the typical disruptions of modern life by the mind-bendingly simple technique of stubbornly refusing to modernise. Instead, some of the Irish clung to an image of themselves as living in a pastoral never-never land full of comely maidens and athletic, morally upright young men. Ireland avoided the upheavals of the Second World War by remaining neutral. It avoided ethnic conflict, at least until quite recently, by being a nation which people abandoned rather than joined. It locked away its unmarried mothers in asylums, sheltered its wife beaters and child abusers from public exposure, and looked the other way while some of its rural population fell through sheer solitude and boredom into mental illness and a slow death of the spirit. Sheer soul-killing tedium, not crime or evil, was for a long time what characterised the country.

Ireland's hidden past is now catching up with it, as women refuse to stay muzzled, paedophile priests are publicly unmasked, immigrants force it to confront its racism, and modernisation is let rip. But throughout all this the country has found a way of co-existing with its old bugbear Britain, rediscovered some of its finest traditional culture, preserved its sense of humour, irony and enjoyment, and found a role for itself on the international stage.

POTATOES

At one point in Irish history, maybe a third of the population, the so-called 'potato people', survived almost entirely on these ingenious vegetables. They depended on it for over 90% of their diet. If that doesn't sound too alluring, one should remember that the potatoes most of the Irish lived on tasted better than they do today. On the whole, the Irish enjoyed their spuds. Potatoes are highly nutritious, with high energy value and low fat content, so that though the Irish were poorly clothed and housed, they were kept warm by all that turf, and mostly well-fed. As long, of course, as the potato crop didn't fail; when it did, the result was widespread famine.

Potatoes were cheap, plentiful, easy to plant, easy to cook, viable in sour, acidic Irish soil, easily accessible, hard to pillage, ready to eat, resistant to disease, and fairly economical of land. Frost is more their enemy than rain, so they're excellently adapted to the country's damp, temperate climate. The downside is that they were hard to store and transport, so that many of the Irish had to endure several months of near-destitution each year between the crops. When this happened, the men would sometimes sail to Britain as temporary labourers, where they would be jeered at as potato-eaters. This was ironic, since the fact that they had no potatoes to eat was why they were in Britain in the first place.

The fact that potatoes are hard to transport accounts for why they spread so rapidly across the whole of the island. They first came to the country in the seventeenth century, as a crop used by the gentry alone; but by the eighteenth century they had become the winter food of some of the poor, and then the apple potato, which was edible all the year round, helped them to become an annual staple. Some of the English regarded the potato as one major cause of Irish backwardness. Growing them didn't require that much labour, so was thought to breed indolence, and they were seen by the English as a less civilised, more bestial diet than grain. So-called cottiers in Ireland rented a small potato patch along with a cabin from their landlord; landless labourers were the lowest of the low, without even a permanent potato patch to call their own. Instead, they hired a patch of ground from a landlord, usually at an exorbitant rent, and grew there the unappetising lumper potato, which required little manuring.

Q

One of the mysteries of the Republic of Ireland is that there is nothing in it of any significance whatsoever beginning with the letter Q.[24] Irish scholars have written books and held conferences on why this is so, and the government has offered a £20,000 reward to anyone who can discover an interesting Irish Q-word. This may be a profitable way to spend your holiday. Some of the Irish have even considered installing Queen Elizabeth as Queen of Ireland, just so they can resolve this pressing problem. They are particularly envious of Northern Ireland, since Belfast has a Queen's university, which gives the North an unfair advantage. The

---

[24] FIF: Though there is a belief that the word 'Quiz' was invented by an eighteenth-century Dublin gent who won a bet that he could introduce a new word into the language by chalking 'Quiz' on walls. Since nobody knew what it meant, the word acquired the meaning it has today.

Irish government has asked for the university to be transferred to Dublin, but Ulster says No.

Others have suggested renaming Dublin 'Quilly' or 'Quantock', or inducing small earthquakes with the aid of dynamite. 'Quaker' is a possibility, since Quakers are greatly respected by the Irish for the help they gave them during the Great Famine. (There are a couple of thousand of them in Ireland today.) But the Catholic bishops have unanimously opposed this proposal. They are also opposed to the suggestion of 'Queer'. We thus pass on rapidly to ...

RTE

Radio Telefís Eireann, the Irish broadcasting system. It is publicly owned, but unlike the BBC carries commercials.[25] Americans settling in for an evening's TV viewing may be dismayed to find that there are only four native TV channels, though you can generally receive English stations as well. There's an Irish-language channel, which has some fine cultural programmes, though watching the soap operas you're glad you don't understand them. Americans might also be disappointed to find that they've seen a lot of the programmes already. Irish television buys a huge amount of material from the States, partly because it lacks resources of its own. The quality of Irish television is not brilliant.

RTE, like some other bits of the Irish mass media, is viewed by the traditional political establishment as full of pinkos, long-haired liberals and gay anarchists. There has been a running battle between sections of the Irish media and the Catholic Church, one which reflects the deep division in

---

[25] FIF: RTE pauses twice a day, at noon and at six p.m., for prayer.

Ireland between traditionalists and progressives. One die-hard member of the *Dáil* grumbled that there was no sex in Ireland until television was let into the place. The single most influential TV programme in the country, Gay Byrne's *The Late Late Show*, is the world's longest running live chat show. It was the first place in Ireland where the tabooed question of sex was publicly aired, and some of the other media have set the pace in shaping a more enlightened public opinion. The leading 'quality' Irish newspaper, the *Irish Times*, has a liberal-Protestant background, and plays something like the serious, high-minded role in the country which the BBC has traditionally played in Britain.[26] In a country which calls itself a democracy, some 90% of Sunday newspapers and 80% of daily ones are owned by one man, Tony O'Reilly.

But the best of Irish broadcasting is to be found in the morning call-in shows on radio, which are models of what socially responsible radio can be. These are not programmes crammed with ads, sound bites, red-neck polemic and mindless music, but places where the nation can talk to itself, discuss its anxieties and opinions, argue fiercely, and laugh at itself into the bargain. Ireland is still a small enough society for this to be possible. The dominant tone of such programmes is friendly (but not hearty), informal (but not cosy), humorous, ironic and socially concerned. For someone from a bigger nation, the sense of community –

---

[26] FIF: The playwright Brendan Behan, whose only resemblance to Adolf Hitler was that he too started off as a house painter, is said to have once had a job painting the *Irish Times* building at a time when he was also employed by the newspaper to write the odd piece for them. Legend has it that he would climb from his ladder through the window when his journalistic services were needed, then climb back again and carry on painting.

which as always in Ireland doesn't exclude sharp clashes of opinion – is very striking. You almost expect an Irish newscaster to announce that there's a loose paving stone on O'Connell Street which you'd better look out for. As in Britain, Irish TV newscasters, reporters and personalities are fairly ordinary-looking men and women, not people who look as though they've strayed off the set of a Hollywood movie or been manufactured entirely out of plastic.

ROUND TOWERS

You'll see quite a few of these in Ireland, slim edifices looking like nuclear missiles built out of stone, usually beside a church. Some Irish scholars used to think that they dated from ancient times, and were built by the Druids or Phoenicians. There were noisy debates about whether they were temples of holy fire, sorcerers' towers, pillars for celestial observation, towers for dancing round in honour of the heavens, or phallic symbols in some ancient fertility cult. Someone even suggested that they were covered in grease by Irish monks, who then spent their days sliding merrily down them. As usual, the truth is rather more prosaic. The towers probably date from the Middle Ages, and were a combination of belfries, look-out tower, storage spaces for precious objects, and hiding places when the enemy was spotted advancing in the middle distance. That's why they have doors a long way off the ground, so that you could disappear into them and pull up the ladder behind you.

Round towers aren't to be confused with Martello towers, squatter structures which you see occasionally on the Irish coast. These date from Napoleonic times, and were built to give warning of a French invasion. One reason why Ireland was important to the English, and worth occupying with its troops, was because it represented its exposed western flank. A crafty foe could use the place to slip into Britain by the back door. The French were England's age-old enemies, and happened like the Irish to be Catholic. An Irish college was established in Paris in the sixteenth century for the education of Irish clerics. Many Irish rebels who fled the country, the so-called 'wild geese', ended up as soldiers in the French army. An alliance between France and Ireland was thus always a threat to England.

This actually came about at the end of the eighteenth century, when the revolutionary United Irishmen invited the equally revolutionary French to invade Ireland and help liberate them from their English masters. But the result was something of a shambles. The French fleet tried to land on the south coast of Ireland and was driven back by bad weather. The United Irish leader Wolfe Tone cut his own throat after capture by the English, but he made a botched job of it and died in agony a long time later. This probably gave some quiet satisfaction to his English enemies, proving that the Irish even made a cock-up of killing themselves. A French army landed in the west of the country and advanced inland, but was disgusted to find their Irish comrades dressed in rags and carrying pitchforks. The rebels were defeated by the English, who then proceeded to torture and massacre them on a large scale. Irish-French co-operation has since produced rather less bloody results in the context of the European Union.

An intriguing footnote to Anglo-French relations was the attempted rescue of Queen Marie Antoinette by an Irishman during the French revolution. He was an officer in the Irish Brigade of the French army, and planned to spring the queen from prison and whisk her off to his house in Dingle. The queen actually agreed, until she learned that her husband

and children were not to accompany her. If she hadn't been so concerned for her family, she might have ended her days watching the sun set over the Dingle peninsula, rather than watching nothing whatsoever because she'd had her head chopped off in Paris.

As well as towers, you'll also see quite a few ruined cabins in Ireland, many of which date from only the last century. They were abandoned when their tenants were driven from the land by hunger, or when they were evicted by the landlord for not paying their rent. Evictions were by no means as common as was once believed, but some 70,000 families were forced from their homes between 1846 and 1853, around the time of the Great Famine. Some landlords seized advantage of the Famine to get rid of their surplus tenants and consolidate their land into larger, more viable units.

As we've already seen, some of the English thought that God in his divine demographic wisdom had decided to save Ireland by killing off a million of its people and driving a few million others into exile. These days, contraception has provided a rather less drastic way of limiting the population. But if some people used to consider that starvation was pleasing to the Almighty, the Catholic Church today seems to think that what really riles him are condoms.

SEAMUS AND SINEAD

Some of the Irish who don't speak their own language have retained it in the forms of their names. It's still very popular in the country to give your child an Irish name, not least because there are some fine ones around. Seamus translates as James, Sinead as Jane, Sean as John, Siobhan (pronounced Shevawn) as Joan, Liam as William, Proinsias as Francis, and Maire as Mary. Padraic (which like most Irish words is not pronounced as it looks) is one of the Irish forms of Patrick. If you dislike your children and want to embarrass them when they go abroad, or even when they step out to the post office, you can always call the boys Maolbheannachta, Toirdealbhach or Mathghamhain, and the girls Aoibheann, Lasairfhiona, or Meadhbh.[27]

SHAMROCK

No such thing, at least from the viewpoint of a botanist. Shamrock just means any of various plants with trifoliate leaves. Its three-in-one form symbolises the Trinity. In the nineteenth century, an Irish botanist had thirty-five specimens of shamrock sent to him for scientific examination from all over the country. They turned out to represent four entirely different plants. Shamrock is green, of course, as befits Ireland, but green has only been the symbolic colour of the country fairly recently. Some scholars think it used to be blue. If you see an Irish person wearing green, remember that it probably has about as much significance as if you saw a Mexican wearing it.

A green flag with a golden harp was for a long time the national symbol of Ireland. Henry VIII added a crown to the harp, just to signify his kingship over the country. Later Irish nationalists sometimes kept the harp but treasonably removed the crown. Towards the end of the eighteenth century in Europe, the colour green became the symbol not

---

[27] FIF: The most common surname in Ireland is Murphy, which in Irish means 'sea hound'. 'Murphies' are also potatoes in Irish slang.

only of Ireland but of Liberty and Revolution in general, symbolising as it did a spring-like renewal of life. At about the same time in Ireland, the colour orange came to represent Protestant loyalty to the English crown and constitution. After Ireland's political union with Britain in 1800, the new national symbol became the Union flag, a bit of which (red on white) was meant to symbolise Ireland because it was thought to be a St Patrick cross. This was considerate of the British, even if they were wrong about what a St Patrick cross looks like. To compound the error, the union flag was (and is) often enough flown upside down.

In the nineteenth century, the green flag with the golden harp went on being used by Irish nationalists, since they objected to the union with Britain. But they also invented their own version of the French tricolour, which was green, white and orange. The white was meant to be a kind of symbolic link between the green (Gaelic-Catholic) and the orange (Northern-Protestant), though some see it as the blank of their mutual incomprehension. This flag flew over Dublin's General Post Office during the Easter Rising in 1916, though there was a green flag beside it, just to keep everyone happy. The tricolour was later to become the official flag of the Irish Republic. In Northern Ireland, it remains the symbol of Catholic nationalism, whereas Protestants fly the Union flag.

SHILLELAGH

A village in County Wicklow. Not a traditional Irish cudgel. There's no ancient Irish weapon of that name, whatever the tourist shops may claim. The village of Shillelagh, a well-forested spot, used to produce oak walking sticks which were sometimes used for fighting; but the blackthorn cudgel sold today as a shillelagh has no tradition behind it at all. Shillelaghs are as fraudulent as the belief that the Irish are a particularly belligerent lot (see VIOLENCE).

SKIES

One of the country's finest features. The subtly, ceaselessly changing skies, light and cloud formations are one of Ireland's delights, and unlike the Giant's Causeway cost nothing to see. Rather less delightful is the fact that the sun appears on average only one day in three. But mild temperatures keep the place green throughout the year, which saves the Tourist Board from having to paint it. The hazy, humid atmosphere of the island mixes, mutes and refracts colours so that a place never quite looks the same.

SPORT

The Irish are in general a physically robust people. Eating nothing but potatoes may have been boring, but potatoes, as we've seen, contain almost all you need for a healthy diet. When he emigrated abroad, the physical strength of the farmer could be adapted to digging canals and laying roads. Combine this stamina with the traditional Irish spirit of daring and physical courage, and the result is a sports-crazed nation of fine sportsmen and sportswomen. In fact sport is the modern version of the old Irish clannishness, popular with a people who enjoy doing things in crowds rather than pursuing solitary pleasures. Though they're also great fishermen and women. In England, fishing is the most popular sport of all, maybe because the English are a more reserved race who enjoy being on their own.

The Irish play soccer, rugby and some cricket, as well as their own traditional games of hurling and Gaelic football, a sort of cross between rugby and football. Hurling is the fastest field game in the world, and camogie is a version of it for women. There are over two hundred and fifty golf courses in Ireland, and horse-racing is a religion for its fans. There can still be some antagonism between English and Irish games, with the more purist of the Irish disdaining rugby and football as imperialist plots against them. The Gaelic Athletic Association, which supervises native Irish sports, is an immensely powerful organisation, second only perhaps to the Catholic Church. Other sports in Ireland include turning signposts around in the countryside to confuse tourists, and a game played by bus drivers, which consists in four buses which were supposed to have arrived at ten minute intervals holding back for an hour and then all arriving together.

TARA

Site of the ancient kings of Ireland in County Meath, and one of traditional Ireland's most sacred symbols. Actually, it's a rather low, inconspicuous-looking hill, quite easy to miss.[28] Another example of the Irish talent for under-statement. You won't find any ruined palaces, though there are some extensive earthworks. This is because there were never any palaces there in the first place. Tara is less a kind of ruined Windsor Castle than a symbol of the spirit of ancient Irish sovereignty. If it doesn't look too imposing

---

[28] FIF: It's said that all four provinces of Ireland can be seen from Tara.

today, that's because it didn't look too imposing in its hey-day either. Some years ago, an eccentric political party had the bright idea of shifting the Irish capital from Dublin to Tara, but the lure of the Dublin pubs proved too much. There's no Temple Bar in Tara, which would have proved a definite drawback.

Tara was really a devious invention of early Irish politicians, who were as cunning then as they are now. It grew out of the idea that Ireland, where political power was divided among many small kingdoms, ought to be bang up-to-date, take a leaf out of the book of other countries and have its own national monarchy. So the politicians persuaded the people that this was exactly what Tara had represented from time immemorial. The only drawback to this theory was that it wasn't true. But the leaders managed to sell this outrageous fiction to their followers, who gullibly swallowed it. For centuries afterwards, Irish scholars wrote solemnly of Tara as the seat of the high kingship of the country, which was about as much of an historical reality as Cinderella. It's as though the US government today decided that the nation needed a Queen Mother, and conned the American people into believing that this is what Meryl Streep had been all along.

Like most myths, however, this one wasn't entirely mythical. There was indeed an important kingship based at Tara, though not one that ruled all Ireland. But it was the centre of sovereignty for some of the northern kingdoms; and when this sovereignty was yielded up to Brian Boru, who came from the southern half of the island, the idea that Tara was now the power-house of the whole country began to catch on. (Brian, by the way, was of the Kennedy clan, and thus a relative of a later political leader.)

Tara is the spot whereon St Patrick is mythically said to have defeated paganism in Ireland. It's also associated with the early bards, and so became a symbol of Irish art. James Joyce once remarked that the quickest way to Tara is the boat to Holyhead, meaning that the surest way to become a great Irish writer was to get out of the place as soon as you can.

TIPPERARY

It's a myth that it's a long way to Tipperary. Nowhere in Ireland is a long way from anywhere else. Tipperary may be a long way from Tibet, but that's the Tibetans' problem. The island as a whole measures around 32,500 square miles, and its widest distance is a mere 189 miles. Its greatest length is only 302 miles. So be careful not to fall off the edge. The place is as far north as Newfoundland, is one of the windiest regions in the world, and in south-western areas it rains two days out of three.

Most of the island consists of an undulating plain of limestone, covered with peat bog and numerous lakes. This is almost completely encircled by a coastal belt of highlands, some of it granite. The mountains of the country are very low, almost never reaching more than 1000 metres. Offshore lie over five hundred islands, of which only sixty-four are inhabited today. In general, the margins of the country are more alluring than the middle. The whole country was covered with ice during the Ice Age, leaving some spectacular valleys, corries, ridges, and mountain lakes. Without the Ice Age, there probably wouldn't be any need for an Irish Tourist Board today.

The central limestone plain, with its luxurious grasslands and rolling cattle farms, is the richest agricultural land, and the place where Irish thoroughbred horses are produced. The farms of the east and south-east, which have the lowest rainfall, grow wheat, barley, potatoes and sugar beet, with yields among the highest in Europe. The south and south-west are mainly milk-producing regions, while to the west of the River Shannon you can find sheep farming, as you can on the hilly areas in general. Some farmers in the west have to struggle hard to survive, even with state support, and migration from the area is heavy.

Ireland became an island before Britain did, which affected its plant and animal life. English animals like moles and weasels don't exist in the country, and there are only two kinds of mice as opposed to four sorts in Britain. Some Irish nationalists regard this as a mark of national shame, and are petitioning the government to introduce more breeds of the beast so they can feel less inferior to their British neighbours. The Irish do have a spotted slug not to be found in many other places, but nationalists regard this as insufficient compensation. They even had to rely on the Normans to introduce the rabbit. On the other hand, there are over four million sheep, which works out at a generous one-and-a-bit for every citizen. Offshore, over twenty species of whale have been found lurking around, along with dolphins and basking sharks. Fortunately for Irish swimmers, the teeth of the basking shark are extremely small. It's a myth that the country has no snakes. Grass snakes are occasionally to be found, carelessly overlooked by St Patrick when he drove the species out of Ireland.[29]

---

[29] FIF: Much of the world's population of Greenland Whitefronted

Ireland is divided into four ancient provinces: Leinster, Munster, Connaught and Ulster. Strangely, however, the Irish word for a province means a fifth. So either the Irish can't count, or they have mislaid one of their provinces in a moment of absent-mindedness. Or perhaps it's just the Irish habit of exaggerating. One solution to the puzzle is that the fifth province consisted of County Meath, which means in Irish 'middle'.

TORIES

In Britain, the word means Conservatives. In traditional Ireland it meant brigands and highwaymen, some of whom were Irish aristocrats who had been dispossessed of their estates and had taken instead to roaming the hills with a pistol. They were Robin Hood figures, shrouded in glamorous mythology. Since they supported the old Gaelic aristocratic order, which the English were busy modernising out of existence, the word 'Tory' came to pass into English political language to mean someone who wants to conserve the past. For present-day opponents of English Tories, the word still means plunder and daylight robbery.

TRAVELLERS

Formerly known as 'tinkers'. There are over twenty thousand of them in Ireland, as well as several thousand in Britain and the States. Travellers are neither Gypsies nor Romanies, who entered Europe from India, but a group

---

geese spends the winter in Ireland. The more artistic of them are exempted from income tax.

native to Ireland and Britain. Some believe that they're the descendants of a caste of craft workers who were ousted from pre-Gaelic Ireland by the arrival of the Gaels. In sixteenth- and seventeenth-century Ireland, professional travellers were often skilled craftsmen, as well as poets, doctors, seers and druids. They traded in finely crafted metalwork, became horse-dealers and tinsmiths, and developed their own distinctive sub-culture and informal economy within Ireland as a whole. Their major meeting places were rural country fairs, nowadays much in decline. In modern times they became dealers in scrap metal, but many of them these days live on social welfare. Travellers don't travel all the time: just under half of them these days are settled on housing sites, often struggling to get by in appalling conditions without adequate facilities.

Travellers are the ultimate scapegoats of Irish society. In a nation traditionally obsessed with owning land, there's little elbow-room for the propertyless. Vigilante groups have attacked them, local authorities have driven them off their land, and keeping them on the move has become a national neurosis. Anti-Traveller racism in Ireland is extremely high, not least since the intimate nature of Irish life makes it hard for outsiders to be invisible. Having been excluded from social facilities, Travelling people are then demonised as dirty, criminal, illiterate spongers on the welfare state. They have a lower life-expectancy than settled people, as well as one of the highest birth rates in the European Union. They also have a high incidence of infantile mortality, and – since Travellers tend to marry within their own group – a history of genetic disorders. The good news is that the Travellers are fighting back, with some eloquent political spokespersons of their own. But with racism steadily rising in Ireland as a whole, the prospects for Travellers are not cheerful.

TREE

There aren't many of these in Ireland, since most of the forests were torn down centuries ago for industrial and military purposes.[30] But 'tree' for some of the Irish is the number which comes after two. Many Irish people pronounce *th* as *t*, influenced by their native language. So 'tree trees' may mean 'three trees' or 'three threes'. 'A great tinker' may mean Plato, not the guy down the road who mends pots and pans. The word 'Thames' might have been specially invented for the Irish, since the *th* is pronounced as *t* anyway. But some of the Irish overcompensate for what they see as a lower-class vulgarity by pronouncing such words as they're written.

To complicate matters, some Irish also pronounce *t* a bit like *th*, saying 'throuble' rather than 'trouble'. The letter *s* at the beginning of a word is pronounced by some Irish people as *sh*, so that 'stick' becomes the Yiddish-sounding 'shtick'. The letter 'aitch', as we've seen, is pronounced 'haitch' in Ireland. If some of the English drop their aitches, the Irish stick one on. Some of the Irish say not 'film' but 'filum', 'mod*r*en' rather than 'modern', and even 'sallat' rather than 'salt'. The Dublin accent is like nothing else in Ireland, indeed like nothing else on earth. To adapt a saying of George Bernard Shaw: the English and the Irish are divided by the same language.

---

[30] FIF: One reason why traditional Irish houses are so shallow – usually only one room deep – was because it was hard to find timber for big crossbeams.

UNIQUENESS

There are several ways in which Ireland is a unique country, not all of them to its credit:

1. It's the most westerly country in Europe. The beautiful Dingle penisular in the west is the nearest point in Europe to North America.

2. Ireland is the only Catholic country in western Europe, if you exclude the officially Catholic but actually godless France.

3. It is the only Celtic nation-state in the world. The other Celtic peoples – Welsh, Manx, Breton, Cornish, Scottish – don't have independent states of their own, though some of them want one.

4. Ireland has the youngest population in Europe. A staggering 44% of the Irish were under 25 in 1991, and about 27% of them were under the age of 14. There are 10,000 or so students packed into Trinity College in the centre of the city. So don't come here if you're feeling your age: people will make it worse by holding doors open for you, or just staring blankly through you at someone their own age.

5. It's the most sparsely populated country in Europe. You can still travel for miles out in the west and see almost nobody, except for other tourists who are seeing almost nobody but you. Oddly, though, Ireland has the highest level of roads in the EU on a *per capita* basis. The Irish writer Samuel Beckett found the country's 'scant population' one of its most charming features, which was a way of saying that he couldn't stand his fellow countrypeople.

6. Ireland is the most centralised country in the European Union. In the Middle Ages, it was just a patchwork of kingdoms with no real political centre, which is why some people think the Irish are natural anarchists. But these days Dublin overshadows everywhere else, and almost one third of a total Irish population of 3.8 million lives there. The capital leaves few real powers to local government. This is deeply resented by the more far-flung regions, who have to consult Dublin over trivial matters they could manage much better themselves. One reason why things in Ireland get done so slowly.

7. It likes to think of itself as the most highly taxed country in Europe, with the highest rate of income tax at around 46%. Whether this is actually the case is another matter

but some think this is another reason why the Irish don't dash to the office at 6.30 in the morning.

8. Ireland is the longest continuously settled nation in north-western Europe. Despite its history of invasion and upheaval, the same people have continued to live in the same place for longer than anywhere else in that part of the globe.

9. Ireland was probably the only place where Christianity was established without bloodshed.

10. More people have probably left Ireland than any other European country.

11. Ireland was the first nation to win political independence in this century. It's the first modern post-colonial society.

12. Sigmund Freud once remarked that the Irish were the only people who couldn't be psychoanalysed. The Irish like to think that this is because they have no need for it; others suggest that it is because they are beyond hope.

13. Along with Spain, Ireland had until fairly recently the highest unemployment rate of the industrialised world.

14. Ireland is the best place on the planet to avoid an earth-quake. No epicentre has ever been recorded there. This may seem a somewhat paranoid reason for settling in the place, but those from San Francisco may find it attractive.

15. It has the highest church attendance of anywhere in western Europe. Catholic Poland outdoes it in the east, but as far as church attendance goes the Polish church has the unfair advantage over Ireland of having been recently persecuted.

16. It has the world's oldest whiskey distillery, established in 1608 at Bushmills on the Antrim coast, but in

production there since the thirteenth century. While Shakespeare was giving the world *King Lear*, the Irish were treating it to the hard stuff. Like Scotch, Irish whiskey is made mainly from malted barley, but whereas Scotch is made in a still which is heated by steam, Irish whiskey is concocted in a different kind of still which is heated by anthracite.

17. Ireland is the first nation to have elected a feminist, Mary Robinson, as head of state. Rumour has it that Queen Elizabeth leads a secret life, hanging around bars in a butch haircut and dungarees, but Buckingham Place denies this. Though they would, wouldn't they?

18. The country has the oldest vernacular literature in Europe, and one of the most richly imaginative.

19. The Irish are the world's greatest tea drinkers, consuming three kilos of tea per capita each year. This puts them well ahead of the English. Tea goes back a long way in Ireland: in fact the daughter-in-law of Milesius, the (mythical) father of the Irish race, was called Tea.

20. Ireland has more dogs per capita than any other EU country. Though the Irish are on the whole much less sentimental about them than are the English, reflecting the difference between a largely rural and a largely urban nation.

VIOLENCE

The Irish are thought to be a notoriously belligerent bunch, forever at each other's throats. Despite the fact that the word 'hooligan' comes from an Irish surname, this is yet another tattered old myth. There was a lot of sporadic rebellion against British rule in the nineteenth century, but probably less violence than there was in Britain itself. There were a number of insurrections against the state, but only one of them, in 1798, resulted in serious bloodshed, and that was mostly because of British brutality. It's true the Irish used to fight among themselves in the old days, partly because they didn't have much else to do other than plant potatoes, which wasn't as exciting as splitting each other's skulls. But these so-called 'faction fights' were more social rituals than vicious conflicts, even if a lot of people got injured or even killed. The Irish have often been a fractious, quarrelsome sort of folk, which perhaps comes from being pent up together on a small island. In a prison camp during the Spanish civil war, where IRA prisoners were housed, there were said to be three factions on the subject of the war: pro-Franco, anti-Franco, and Brendan Behan.

As we've seen, there was a bloody civil war in the early 1920s between those who accepted the Anglo-Irish Treaty and those who rejected it. An Abbey Theatre play produced during the conflict had a programme note assuring the audience that all sounds of gunfire were from the stage, and that they should keep their seats. But Ireland has never gone to war with any other nation since ancient times, though they have fought a lot in other people's battles. The Irish navy is so small that you could fit it on a boating lake. The only smaller one is the Swiss. (The Swiss don't have any coastlines.) Ireland was neutral in the Second World War, and since then has kept its distance from military alliances like NATO. Its international standing comes not from throwing its armed might around the world, but from its cultural achievements.

In our own time, Irish troops have made a major contribution to UN peace-keeping missions, and the country has an enlightened track record at the United Nations on opposing militarism and defending human rights. Despite their traditional lack of affluence, the Irish are famous for their charitable contributions to alleviating poverty and suffering throughout the world. They have done this both by money and man-power, the latter in the form of missionaries. Some think that this is because of their own experience of famine, but it might simply be that, as one of the most Christian nations on earth, they are brought up with a sense of moral responsibility. In a country without much tradition of civic responsibility, religion has valuably filled the gap, despite the way in which a rigidly authoritarian church has blighted and damaged so many Irish lives. It's probably because of this religious upbringing that significantly more Irish than other Europeans believe that you should love and respect your parents regardless of their faults. Or so the opinion polls tell us.

In Ireland as elsewhere, drug-related crime is ominously increasing. On one estimate, Dublin's heroin problem is proportionately as big as New York's. There are urban wastelands which breed drug mafias and gangland shootings. Ireland is a rougher, more violent place than it was. The crime level in general has shot up dramatically since the 1960s – though in 1996 there were only 42 murders, a figure Americans in particular are likely to find quaint in the extreme. As in Britain, a murder will make the headlines, which can hardly be said of Miami. (Car accidents make the headlines too.) Americans who stay in Ireland for a period of time gradually learn different bodily habits. Having realised that they're unlikely to be mugged in Mullingar, the tense, vigilant body of the New Yorker begins gradually to relax. This doesn't mean that it's safe to stroll in Phoenix Park at night, or even sometimes by day. The country has become a lot less safe, though it's still a good deal safer than some. You have much less chance of being shot in Belfast than in Chicago.

Like the British police, the Irish police force, known as the *Garda Siochana*, are unarmed. Only plain-clothes detectives carry guns.[31] Not long ago, Ireland had the lowest homicide rate in Europe, as well as fewer assaults per head of the population. Its prisons, however, are seriously overcrowded. There are around 10,500 police officers in the country, including a few hundred female officers who have finally, after much huffing and puffing from their seniors, been allowed to desecrate their womanhood by wearing trousers rather than skirts. Being a police officer is regarded as a plum job for unemployed youths, and there's no shortage of recruits despite the lengthy period of training.

Opinion polls suggest that the Irish people hold their police force in fairly high regard – certainly more so than most European nations, though the *Garda* have their bent coppers and resident thugs like any other force. The British are much less inclined to revere their police than they used to be, partly because of a series of grotesque miscarriages of justice involving Irishmen wrongly convicted of terrorism. The *Garda* now have a special Drugs Squad, whose services are becoming more necessary daily, and a Fraud Squad, also necessary given the dubious behaviour of some Irish banks. You can find plenty of Neighbourhood Watch schemes in the country, which means that your neighbours watch from their windows while someone breaks down your front door and runs off with your video recorder.

---

[31] FIF: From 1970 to 1990, only twelve police officers were murdered in the country.

Irish police are banned from taking strike action, though recently, while pressing for higher pay, 80% of them reported sick and then joined a huge demonstration in the centre of Dublin. Medical authorities are still trying to figure out how so many police officers could have fallen ill at exactly the same time.

WAKE

Known elsewhere as a funeral. The Irish are as expert in making a festival out of death as they are in making merry in life. At a wake, the corpse is laid out on public view in the family home, and neighbours drop by to commiserate with the relatives, drink, eat, talk, play music and sometimes dance. The whole event might go on for several days. This still happens in Ireland, though mostly in the countryside. It's basically a pagan idea, as much of Irish popular culture used to be. Celtic spirituality, pagan practices and Christian beliefs were traditionally blended together. Wakes reflect a fear of death: you give the corpse a good send-off in case it comes back to haunt you. But they also reflect the belief that life and death are bound up with each other. The Irish don't try to tidy death away, like some other nations.

Wakes in the old days could get fairly riotous, given the amount of alcohol that was sunk. You might put a bottle of whiskey in the corpse's hand, stick a pipe in its mouth, or even, if things got really wild, drag it around the dance floor. This was a sign of friendship to the dead person, rather than of disrespect. It was an attempt to make up to them for the misfortune of being dead. When someone emigrated to the States, an 'American wake' would be held for them. A lot of Irish emigrants did in fact see going to Britain or the States as a bit like going to heaven, though some of them no doubt found them fairly hellish.

Popular culture in Ireland in the old days could be quite a carnival. On festive occasions, people might engage in nudity, cross-dressing, mock marriages, sexual horseplay. Some of their games mocked the clergy, and some even mocked Christ. The eighteenth century poet Brian Merriman wrote a bawdy, rollicking poem in Irish called 'The Midnight Court', in which the poet, a bachelor, falls asleep and has a dream. A monstrous female fairy appears and hauls him off to appear before the Queen's court of women, on the charge that he persists in being celibate while Irish women are pining for lack of sexual fulfilment. The women complain about the shortage of suitable marriage partners, and the distressing nature of unions between lusty young women and wizened old men. On behalf of her womenfolk, the Queen finds the poet guilty of anti-social celibacy and proposes to punish him, whereupon, luckily for him, he wakes up.

The Irish were traditionally an iconoclastic bunch, and their popular culture could be rough, knockabout and exuberant. But the Great Famine last century killed a lot of it off, though it had been declining even before then. The church was always hostile to these festivities, seeing in them a threat to its own power; and Ireland after the Famine was on the whole a more sedate, respectable place. But you can find traces of this satirical culture in Ireland today, in Irish irreverence and debunkery. They don't drag corpses out on the dance floor any more, but they might drag *you* out if they're feeling feisty enough.

WEST

The west of Ireland is one of the most charming places in the world, not just in Europe. Its people are for the most part as courteous and humane as myth would have it. I once stepped into a small shop in a village in the west to ask the way to the bank. They gave me directions, and as I was entering the bank they were phoning it to make sure that I'd arrived. It's never happened to me in Tokyo.

The tourist, however, sees only the breathtaking appearances: the cliffs of Moher, the bizarre lunar landscape of the Burren, the rocky fields of Connemara. But the most spectacular parts of Ireland are also on the whole the poorest. Behind the seductive appearances, the west of Ireland is in deep trouble, with parts of it dying on its feet. For some years, it has been emptying like a burning building, as its people flock into the cities from its infertile land and unprofitable farms. Whole settlements have slowly collapsed, leaving behind them lonely men and women with a disturbingly high rate of mental illness. More men than women, in fact, which reverses the trend elsewhere in Europe. Local industries have been ousted by multinational operations, agribusiness has crushed a lot of small farms, and many small businesses have faded away. The west is an ecological time-bomb, its salmon poisoned by industrial chemicals, its mountains chewed bare by overstocked sheep, the whole region a victim of minimal planning controls and ill-managed development. There is, however, no truth in the rumour that sheep farmers out west, who receive a grant per head of sheep, are painting the rocks in their field white so that they may be mistaken for sheep when viewed from an overhead satellite.

The good news is that the west is fighting back, full of creative projects and community spirit. Galway, for example, has leapt from being a sleepy rural backwater to a glamorous centre of modern industry, New Age drop-outs, artists and Irish speakers. But get out west as quick as you can before they plonk a supermarket on the cliffs of Moher.

The west of Ireland has been seen often enough as a timeless peasant world where Ireland can be encountered in its purest, most primeval state. This, in fact, is yet another myth. Large swathes of the west were only permanently settled in the late eighteenth and early nineteenth centuries, as the country's bulging population spilled over to huddle on the western seaboard. Around this time the economy of the west was booming, and you couldn't see the scenery for the masses of people. Far from being some Celtic Garden of Eden, it was a bustling, fairly go-ahead sort of region. The idea of the west as an ancient paradise in which time has been suspended didn't fully develop until the end of the last century. Like most dreams of primitive rural paradises, it was the fantasy of townsfolk.

WILDE

Famous Irish writer. A fashionable figure about Dublin, Wilde was a collector of Irish folklore and an eminent Gaelic scholar. Despite being known as the dirtiest man in Dublin because of his shabby appearance, he was one of the most distinguished physicians in Ireland, and was appointed Surgeon Oculist to Queen Victoria in Ireland. Something of a philanderer, he is said to have operated on the eyes of the king of Sweden, and when the king was temporarily blinded, seduced his queen. A condition of the inner ear is still known today as Wilde's syndrome. He married the flamboyant Jane

Elgee, a fiery nationalist poet and rebel who called herself 'Speranza'. She threw lavish parties and lived in a world of exotic fantasy. She once stood up in a courtroom and demanded to be tried in place of her Fenian colleague in the dock.

They also had a son called Oscar.

WOMEN

Not all Irish women are Grace O'Malleys, but the typical image of them is as strong, shrewd, practical and affirmative. This may be because they've been saddled with so many hopeless men. For all his occasional bluster and bragging, the Irish man has often been seen as emotionally retarded and much given to sentimentality, perhaps because late marriage made him dependent too long on his mother or 'mammy'. Irish women, by contrast, tend to be deeply unsentimental and unromantic, as women needed to be in a rural culture where they shouldered a lot of the responsibility. The blushing English rose doesn't grow readily in Irish soil.

Women in Celtic society had an unusual degree of freedom. They could divorce their husbands and wield political power. But under the common law imposed on Irish society by the English, a married woman was in effect the property of her husband, who could do with her what he pleased short of killing, selling or seriously injuring her. Even so, visitors to Ireland in the eighteenth century were struck by the free-and-easy sexual talk of the women, as well as by an air of independence which is still in evidence today.[32] In modern times, Ireland has been a highly patriarchal society, and the club of male celibates known as the Catholic Church has done its best to keep women in their place. In 1948, the Irish state seriously considered banning young women from emigrating, long before the Berlin wall had been dreamt up by the East Germans. Women's role was to stay at home, bear as many children as possible, and be shining examples of Irish modesty and self-sacrifice.

The index entry for 'Women' in an edition of the Irish constitution reads: 'See Family, Sex'. A law of 1925 prohibited divorce, while one two years later virtually banned women from jury service. In 1935, the sale, advertising and importation of contraceptives was forbidden, and the Catholic bishops condemned modern dancing and 'immodest' fashions in female dress. Some clerics considered Irish dancing just about acceptable because it was too laborious to last very long. Married women were banned from recruitment to the public service, and abortion was not even discussible. For almost 30 years, women in Ireland were deprived of legal aid and unemployment benefit; there was no financial help for single mothers or deserted wives, and no protection for battered ones. Until 1965, a wife could be totally disinherited by her husband. Apart from nursing and domestic service, teaching and secretarial work, there were very few careers open to women.

Much of this is now changing, in one of the most deep-seated social revolutions the country has ever witnessed. Joining the European Union meant that Ireland was forced

---

[32] FIF: Up to the twelfth century in Ireland, marriage was an annual contract, and you could divorce your spouse by walking out on February 1.

to introduce laws on equal pay, a measure which the Irish government of the day tried to block. Even so, Irish women are twice as likely as men to be in low-paid jobs. The number of women in work has increased fourfold since the 1960s. By some measurements, however, the country still has one of the lowest rates of female labour in the western world. Despite this, about the same number of the Irish agree with the idea of working mothers as in any other European nation, so it's a myth that the Irish are especially conservative in family matters.

Contraception is now plentifully available, though only after a fierce struggle during which feminists took the train to Belfast, bought contraceptives there and returned to Dublin to brandish them defiantly in the faces of an embarrassed bunch of police officers. Contraception only became legal in 1980, and then only for married couples. Family size fell between 1960 and 1990 from about five to two children. Today, around 18% of all births in Ireland are outside marriage. Divorce has just come on the statute books. A large majority of Irish people are firmly opposed to abortion on demand, and a smaller number to abortion in any circumstances. To have an abortion, an Irishwoman must travel to Britain, and several thousand of them do so each year. This is unlikely to change for some time, given the strength of the church and of popular opinion.

Women have by no means swept all before them. Ireland today is a deeply divided society on these questions, as traditional values fight it out with progressive ones. Divorce, for example, got through only by the skin of its teeth. Rural women in particular have a hard time, marooned from social services and doing much of the farm work with scant recognition. Some features of the old Ireland may be dead and buried, but morally and psychologically speaking the place is still much in evidence. There's a refreshing new open-mindedness, but also a sense of spiritual drift and anxiety. As one commentator has put it, Ireland is now in the process of breaking up and selling off all existing beliefs. It's a nation caught on the hop between the traditional and the modern, between the Bishop of Rome and the Treaty of Rome.

On being elected as Ireland's first woman President, Mary Robinson remarked that 'the hand that rocks the cradle has rocked the system'. As a liberal-minded lawyer who had battled for women's rights, Mary Robinson's Presidency came to symbolise for many of her compatriots the new, enlightened Ireland, with its emphasis on cultural diversity, its cosmopolitan vision and concern for the dispossessed. Even so, many Irish women remain stoutly conservative in their views; the battle between traditionalists and modernisers is by no means the same in Ireland as the strife between men and women. Nor, for that matter, is it necessarily one between countryside and city. But the new President is also a woman, Mary MacAleese, and she's the first President of the Republic to hail from the North, which may be a good omen for the future of this divided island.

X-RATED

Ireland has a dismal record of censorship. There used to be a body known as the Committee on Evil Literature, whose job was to keep out any books the bishops didn't agree with.

This usually meant books the bishops didn't understand.[33] The church preferred books with titles like *What To Do on a Date*, which solemnly advised young people to go for a stroll in a crowded street and discuss some intimate subject like international politics. One early Irish film censor, when asked if he knew anything about cinema, replied 'No, but I know the ten commandments'. Sex was seen as an English conspiracy to pollute virginal Irish minds. It was the English who introduced the habit of copulation to the country; before then, Irish children had been born of prayer. These days the censorship has been relaxed, though Ireland is one of the very few democratic countries today in which books can be censored by law. Only a few decades ago, the distinguished Irish novelist John McGahern was dismissed from his job as a schoolteacher for writing novels which mentioned masturbation.

As far as cinema goes, you can see the sort of steamy films you can view elsewhere, though some films are occasionally cut or banned. One casualty of this enlightenment is that soft porn has begun to creep into a country which previously kept it out. You can now find *Playboy* in Irish shops, along with a number of sex shops. There used to be a red light district in the centre of Dublin, in which around sixteen hundred prostitutes were crowded into an area of half a dozen streets, but some Irish say the district was used only by British soldiers. If you believe that, you'll

---

[33] FIF: James Joyce's novel *Ulysses* was never banned in Ireland, despite being the most sexually explicit piece of writing ever to have been produced by the country up to that point. Books were only banned if they were reported to the censors, and nobody reported this one. Perhaps because nobody understood it enough even to realise that it should be censored.

have no problem in believing in leprechauns. Prostitutes still ply their illegal trade in shadowy corners of Dublin, but in general it's a city without sleaze.

What the Irish keep free of censorship is the language in which they discuss their opinions with each other. Public debate in the country can be vicious, abusive and highly personal, though all this can oddly co-exist with chumminess. Faction fighting, in which rival groups in traditional rural Ireland belaboured each other with clubs, has now given way to intensive in-fighting over opinions. In a country where most of the opinion-formers were probably at college with each other, personalities bulk large in conflicts of ideas. Irish fractiousness is the flip side of Irish intimacy. It's a more face-to-face culture than Britain, but for the same reason a more querulous one. Intellectual life, in this eloquent, combative, self-involved culture, is at once vigorous and claustrophobic. As far as intellectual debate goes, some of the Irish have no manners at all. Some arguments in Ireland have been declared invalid on the grounds that they were based on licensed premises.

YEATS, WILLIAM BUTLER

An Irish poet. Yeats believed in fairies, leprechauns, magic, spiritualism, aristocrats, astral bodies, reincarnation, violence, elitism, dictatorship, and forcibly stopping the poor from breeding. He lived in a tower and thought that spirits dictated his poems to him. There have been other Irish writers whose work was dictated by spirits, but these were of the alcoholic rather than angelic kind. Yeats didn't like democracy, strong women, modern life, or people who told him he was talking a lot of nonsense. He was turned down for a professorship at Trinity College because he misspelt the word 'professor' in his letter of application. One of the great mysteries of Ireland is that, despite all this, he is one of the greatest poets of the English language.

ZOOLOGICAL GARDENS, DUBLIN

Not really worth a visit, but what other Z-word can *you* think of?

*

So there we are. The Irish playwright George Bernard Shaw once remarked that to learn something feels at first like losing something. But you can't learn about Ireland without shedding a few myths. In the folk tales, the fairies sometimes spirit away a real child and leave a fairy child in its place. This book has tried to do the opposite, spiriting away a few fairy-tales and substituting a piece of reality. The bad news is that Ireland has no leprechauns, hardly any donkeys, few Irish speakers, a decaying countryside, too much traffic, steep income tax, *Playboy*, a high cost of living, massive unemployment in some areas, untidy streets, and racial tension. It also takes its time to fix your plumbing. Nobody says 'begorrah', taxi-drivers don't suddenly burst out into ancient Irish poetry, Guinness is no longer Irish, and there's nothing beginning with Q. The good news is that the Irish are a good-humoured, vivacious, hospitable people, with a magnificent culture and one of the most beautiful countries on earth. Come on now, isn't that a fair exchange?